Pastor Arni Jacobson is an exceptional friend, both personally and to the City of Green Bay. Few can match the extraordinary abilities he has displayed in transforming the lives of those to whom he ministers. Pastor Jacobson is highly respected throughout Northeast Wisconsin and has proven highly effective in leading area residents to a deeper personal relationship with Christ, prioritizing Him and their faith first in their lives. Upon his move to Salt Lake City, Utah, I was proud to present him with a key to the City of Green Bay. Much as I value Pastor Jacobson's instructive writings, I eagerly anticipate reading *The Favor Factor*.

—James J. Schmitt
Mayor, Green Bay, WI

Favor opens doors of influence and opportunity. Arni is a man who has favor and understands favor. It's God's favor that gives my friend "flavor"!

—Dick Bernal
Founder and Senior Pastor
Jubilee Christian Center, San Jose, CA

Arni is a rock-solid family man and an engaging teacher; he is absolutely passionate about reaching others with God's promise of salvation. His teaching is timely and undoubtedly

Spirit directed. I know you will really enjoy the message of this book.

—T. Pepper Burruss
Green Bay Packers Head Athletic Trainer
and Physical Therapist

The Favor Factor is refreshingly profound and practical and leaves people wanting more. I excitingly endorse the message in this book for anyone who is looking for *favor* in their lives.

—Dale Oquist
Senior Pastor, Evergreen Christian Community
Olympia, WA

Favor is what we must all have to live a satisfying and blessed life. Rather than succumbing to the common notion that favor is what happens to a select few, Arni shares practical principles on how to discover the "favor factor" in the practice of life.

—Steve Riggle
Senior Pastor
Grace Community Church, Houston, TX
President, Christian Evangelistic Association

Pastor Arni Jacobson changed our lives several years ago when he brought us to accept Christ as our Savior. Up until then, we had written off organized religion for almost thirty years. Arni has an incredible passion for leading others to Christ. He, his wife, Jan, and their family remain wonderful friends to my wife, Cathy, and myself. I know Arni, and I know this book will be brilliant.

—GARY TONN
Founder and President
Tonn's, Inc., a franchisee of Taco Bell
Green Bay, WI

During your lifetime, there are many people who will walk in and out of your life, but only a choice few will leave footprints of love, hope, and encouragement on your soul. Pastor Arni Jacobson is that kind of person. He is a dynamic, visionary person with powerful leadership skills. Helping people find Christ is a priority in his life—from well-known sports personalities to a discouraged waitress who just needs some hope. Pastor Arni knows what to say. *The Favor Factor* touched my heart. This book is hope and encouragement and winning people to Christ. Everyone can benefit from this book, regardless of your religious affiliation. It's one of those MUST-READ books that I am putting on my Web site. This book honors God in every way!

—KEN GAUB
Ken Gaub Worldwide Ministries
Yakima, WA

THE
FAVOR FACTOR

THE
FAVOR FACTOR

ARNI JACOBSON

with

ROBERT MIMS

Charisma
HOUSE
A STRANG COMPANY

Most STRANG COMMUNICATIONS/CHARISMA HOUSE/
SILOAM/FRONTLINE/REALMS products are available at
special quantity discounts for bulk purchase for sales
promotions, premiums, fund-raising, and educational
needs. For details, write Strang Communications/
Charisma House/Siloam/FrontLine/Realms, 600
Rinehart Road, Lake Mary, Florida 32746, or telephone
(407) 333-0600.

THE FAVOR FACTOR by Arni Jacobson with Robert Mims
Published by Charisma House
A Strang Company
600 Rinehart Road
Lake Mary, Florida 32746
www.charismahouse.com

Scripture quotations marked KJV are from the King James Version of the Bible.

Cover Design: studiogearbox.com
Executive Design Director: Bill Johnson

Library of Congress Cataloging-in-Publication Data

Jacobson, Arni.
  The Favor factor / by Arni Jacobson. -- 1st ed.
      p. cm.
  Includes bibliographical references.
  ISBN 978-1-59979-098-5 (casebound)
  1. Nehemiah (Governor of Judah) 2. Grace (Theology)
3. Spiritual life. 4. Christian life. I. Title.
  BS580.N45J33 2007
  222'.806--dc22

                                        2007003595

First Edition

07 08 09 10 11 — 987654321
Printed in the United States of America

*I dedicate this book to my family—
my wife, Jan; my son, Chad, his wife,
Amanda, and their two sons, Ethan and
Collin; my daughter, Brooke,
and her husband, Josh.*

Acknowledgments

I would like to acknowledge my friend, Bob Mims, who took my sermons and my thoughts and helped me birth this book.

Give your servant success today by granting him favor in the presence of this man.

—NEHEMIAH 1:11

Contents

THE FAVOR FACTOR

*Ancient wisdom today for God's
"assigned advantage"*

T WAS A very cold winter's day in Green Bay, Wisconsin, and the polar jet stream was doing its best to bring a little bit of the Arctic Circle over Lake Michigan. When I opened the garage door to begin my usual morning jog, I was driven back by a frigid blast.

"No," I decided. "I'm not going out there today." I had a treadmill in the recreation room of our basement. I had already done my morning devotional, so as I closed the garage door against the subfreezing wind, I looked forward to firing up my exercise machinery, turning on the television, and watching my favorite workout time show—ESPN *SportsCenter*.

I grabbed the remote and clicked. Nothing. Maybe the battery had finally given out. "No problem," I thought, walking over to the TV and pushing the power button—and, again, nothing.

I tried both again, getting frustrated that the remote, the TV, or both were broken and I'd have to endure my run without the pleasant distraction of the world of sports.

"Well, I guess I'll just have to pray...get myself through this," I mused. At least the treadmill worked, and so I began to run and open my spirit to God. Then He began to pour things into my heart; the conduit was what had been a routine devotional stop in the Book of Nehemiah.

But now, this was no longer merely an everyday scriptural study. The words, the heart of the author, a Jewish slave boy who had risen to a position of power and trust in the Persian Empire, burned in my thoughts. My heart, mind, and spirit had been captured by a prayer offered in seemingly hopeless circumstances and great risk almost twenty-six hundred years ago. It was a prayer that was much more than something muttered by rote, but a petition that epitomizes that rare mix of desperation and trust that is faith:

> "O LORD, God of heaven, the great and awesome God, who keeps his covenant of love with those who love him and obey his commands, let your ear be attentive and your eyes open to hear the prayer your servant is praying before you day and night for your servants, the people of Israel. I confess the sins we Israelites, including myself and my father's house, have committed against you. We have acted very wickedly toward you. We have not obeyed the commands, decrees and laws you gave your servant Moses.
>
> "Remember the instruction you gave your servant Moses, saying, 'If you are unfaithful,

> I will scatter you among the nations, but if you return to me and obey my commands, then even if your exiled people are at the farthest horizon, I will gather them from there and bring them to the place I have chosen as a dwelling for my Name.'
>
> "They are your servants and your people, whom you redeemed by your great strength and your mighty hand. O Lord, let your ear be attentive to the prayer of this your servant and to the prayer of your servants who delight in revering your name. Give your servant success today by granting him favor in the presence of this man."
>
> I was cupbearer to the king.
>
> —NEHEMIAH 1:5–11

As I ran, the rhythm of my feet on the rolling tread and hum of the machine's electric motor faded, and truths scrolled into my mind; something important was suddenly coming together. I was excited. I realized it was one of those precious, crystal clear moments of teaching from the heart of God to the soul of one of His servants.

I had to write these thoughts down. So I turned off the treadmill, and soon I had a pen in hand. The Holy Spirit gave me seven specific ways God had used Nehemiah, each of them pointing to what I've felt led to call "the favor factor."

1. Give God the credit.
2. Keep God's Word as the centerpiece of your life.
3. Maintain a tender heart toward the Lord.
4. Keep your spiritual house clean.
5. Don't forsake the house of God.
6. Keep God's commands.
7. Keep your family pure.

I jumped back on the treadmill, finished my run, showered, and returned to the rec room. Curious, I picked up the remote.

Click. The TV came on instantly. I thought, "God, You interrupted that signal so You could share with Your servant these truths that I can now share with my congregation!"

In seven messages that followed, I did. And now I can share the same eternal insights with you in this little but powerful book that God began to unravel for me on a cold Wisconsin winter's day.

Let's take a look at those concluding words of Nehemiah's straightforward prayer again:

> O Lord, let your ear be attentive to the prayer of this your servant and to the prayer of your servants who delight in revering your name. Give your servant success today by granting him favor in the presence of this man.

Bless me. Why are we so reluctant to ask God to bless us? I'm convinced that God really does want to bless each of us; it is not selfish at all to pray that from your heart: "God, will You bless me?"

Nehemiah was not afraid to ask for blessing, specifically praying for success and for favor.

I have always been interested in that word—*favor*. *Merriam-Webster's Collegiate Dictionary* defines it as "friendly regard shown toward another especially by a superior." My Nehemiah-influenced definition? "Assigned advantage."

Be attentive to the prayer of Your servant. Another interesting word—*servant.* Not a slave, but a servant who does not have his own agenda but God's; a lifestyle that is totally immersed in the will of God and what God would have him or her to be.

If we can make that kind of commitment and then pray, God takes notice. "Let your ear be attentive...to this your servant." And then? Nehemiah adds all of us too into his prayer—"servants who delight in revering your name."

Revere the name of the Lord. This means to treasure it, honor it, lift it up in our lives, and make it our banner and our life's light. The name of Jesus should be revered by Christians. It is a name we should be excited about, in awe of. You can do great things in that name.

Nehemiah's prayer and this little book exploring its spiritual riches have the ability to change the course of your life for the better. It is a simple prayer, but the decisions that go with it—choices of integrity that touch every arena of your life—can bring you to a place of favor and influence at home, at work, in church, and even in the world at large.

We need to be shining examples. Nehemiah was, and he won God's favor—the Lord's assigned advantage.

> FAVOR—*"friendly regard shown toward another especially by a superior." My Nehemiah-influenced definition?* "Assigned advantage."

As we explore the concept and power of having the favor of heaven permeating your life in all its aspects, I promise you will grow to appreciate more than ever the blessings you have already received—even the miracles that have been your living milestones, though perhaps not recognized until now.

My own story with Christ actually began with what most people would see as a tragedy; I know that for a time I certainly did. How would you react to news that your beloved sister, a vibrant young woman pregnant with her third child and with everything to live for, had terminal Hodgkin's disease?

Judith Ann Doxtater had gone into the hospital in 1963, concerned about a small lump on her neck that would not go away. A biopsy tested positive for Hodgkin's, and doctors determined it was advanced too far for much hope.

At best, they said, the most aggressive treatments available at the time would give Judy two more years of life.

It was devastating news, and yet God would be glorified in ways no one—not Judy; not her husband, Darrell; and not their little girl, Renee, who would have so little time with her mother—could imagine.

In the other bed in that hospital room where my sister heard her death sentence was Millie Scott, a Christian woman who shared her compassion—and testimony—with Judy. Millie invited my sister to visit First Assembly of God Church in Kenosha, Wisconsin, and hear Rev. John Wilkerson speak.

Judy took her up on the invitation and gave her life to Christ as a result of Wilkerson's salvation message. She lived almost four more years, double what doctors had said. More importantly, in those years my sister lived a lifetime of service to the Lord:

she personally brought more than one hundred people into that church to hear the gospel.

Three days before Judy died, she added my parents to the kingdom. At her funeral service, the church was so crowded that there was standing room only. The funeral procession to the cemetery stretched for miles.

God had begun to work on me through my sister, too. I was moved by the funeral message, which included the words from 2 Timothy 4:6–7:

> For I am already being poured out like a drink offering, and the time has come for my departure. I fought a good fight, I have finished the race, I have kept the faith.

That day, I had no doubt that she was in heaven. Still, I was not quite to the point of surrendering my life to Christ; the Holy Spirit had some soul tenderizing to do.

It was four months later, on January 3, 1967, that I embraced that same assurance my sister had, and I knew that I too would some day see Judy again. In a Howard Johnson's restaurant in Chicago while dining with the same Pastor Wilkerson, I asked Christ to become my Savior and Lord.

In a way, I may have been Judy's final triumph—and she would have loved it. Shortly before she died, she had told my older brother, Dave, that she could believe God could save anyone but her cruising, boozing, and indifferent brother Arni.

> *If you are willing to open up to others, the Lord will give you the opportunities.*

But she never gave up. To the end, Judy was constantly sharing Christ, her urgency no doubt fueled by the winding down of her time on Earth. I stubbornly maintained a disinterested demeanor, but the seed she was planting found deep, fertile soil that led to Pastor Wilkerson's harvest a few months later.

Instantly, I became overwhelmed with a hunger to see people come to Christ. I dropped out of college, holding jobs in sales and as a technical clerk for a heavy equipment company while growing as a new Christian. My desire to witness only grew, and I felt called to the pulpit. In 1972, I graduated from

Central Bible College in Springfield, Missouri, and entered the ministry with my new bride, Jan.

If Millie Scott had not shared her testimony and that invitation with my sister, offering a hand of love and friendship at that critical crossroads of her life, how many of those more than one hundred souls—including my family and me—would today face an eternity separated from Christ?

If you are willing to open up to others, the Lord will give you the opportunities. I found that out some years ago, when what seemed like another aggravating flight delay turned into another soul won for Christ.

On that hot August day in Chicago, our plane was moving toward the runway when the flight attendant's voice came over the intercom: the captain, concerned about the added weight humidity was adding to the aircraft, was returning to the terminal. Some passengers would have to depart before it was considered safe to take off. Jan and I volunteered, being rewarded with four extra tickets and assignment to a later flight.

Well, the next flight was overbooked. We again volunteered to wait and received four more free tickets. Reassigned once more, we finally boarded our flight but had to sit separately. I sat next to a businessman.

Since it was a Saturday and I was to preach the next day, I was looking over my notes and reading my Bible. Noticing this, my companion asked what I did for a living. "I'm a pastor," I answered. He then asked what denomination. I told him, naming the evangelical Christian church organization with which I was then affiliated.

A tear welled up in his eye. He told me that was the same denomination his sister had belonged to. She had died two years before—from Hodgkin's disease, the same cancer that had taken my sister's life.

As we talked and I gently prodded, it was clear he had not asked Christ to be his Savior. I asked him if his sister ever mentioned her relationship with the Lord. He pulled out a letter his sister had sent him before she had died; she had told him about his need to place his trust in Jesus, even including a version of the sinner's prayer of repentance.

"Have you prayed this prayer?" I inquired. He said he didn't understand it, so I explained the good news of Jesus's life, death, resurrection, and offer of forgiveness of sin. Moments later, we were praying that prayer together. Somewhere over the plains of the Midwest, he became a believer.

Just as I had done because of my own sister's prayer for me, this man had come to a saving knowledge of Christ because of his sister's willingness to reach out to her errant brother. God had arranged a day of oppressive, humid weather to put me in the right spot at the right time to see one of His children set free.

There are many more stories like Millie's, like my sister's, and like my own that illustrate the powerful reality of seeking and exercising God's favor in your life. Favor amplifies your gifts, and as long as you use those gifts and talents to advance the kingdom of heaven, the Lord has promised to pour out His blessings.

I am convinced that the reason I have found favor in my life is that I have had a heart for seeing people come to Christ. It is why we exist here as God's children, after all, but somewhere along the path we have lost the reason for our existence.

> *I am convinced that the reason*
> *I have found favor in my life is that*
> *I have had a heart for*
> *seeing people come to Christ.*

I pray this book will be useful at all levels of your spiritual journey. There are lessons and encouragement from the heart of God for all—for those just beginning to feel that emptiness inside that only Christ can fill, to those who find themselves at a crossroads in their walk with the Lord, and even to those who have served the Lord for decades and desire a deeper, more blessed and mature experience.

Whatever your circumstances, be assured they are neither the last stop nor the ultimate destination of your walk with the Savior.

And, as Nehemiah shows us, the blessings of God are limited only by the scope of our vision and our willingness to believe and obey.

Chapter 2

A CUPBEARER TO THE KING

*Nehemiah's grief, prayer, and
the depth of God's answers*

EHEMIAH'S NATION WAS as broken and scattered as were the walls of its once rich, powerful, and envied capital, Jerusalem. Nebuchadnezzar II had seen to that nearly one hundred fifty years before, stripping the gold and silver from Solomon's temple and then destroying the jewel of Judah. The City of David had been razed, the sputtering candle of the once-blessed kingdom of Israel snuffed.

Some hope for Israel had stirred when the Persians swallowed up Babylon and its vassals. King Cyrus had allowed a remnant of the Jews to return to their ancient city, and then Darius had given his permission to rebuild the temple, a task completed some sixty years before. But that bright spot in the Jewish exile was not long in being overshadowed by the politics of the Medo-Persian Empire and the violence of the Samaritans, who resented any revival of Jerusalem or the power of the Jewish people.

Now, Artaxerxes Longimanus was on the throne. His two decades as ruler had been perplexing and a blessing at the same time. Early in his reign, the great king had, after all, listened to false reports of pending rebellion and ordered all work on the rebuilding of the walls of Jerusalem to cease. Having successfully deceived the king, the empire's chancellor over Samaria and his secretary, Shimshai, had delighted in issuing and implementing the edict with special zeal.

The two had ridden in with troops, burned the gates, and toppled much of three years' hard work.

But at the same time, Artaxerxes had taken a liking to Nehemiah. The king, whose domain stretched over most of the planet, trusted the young Jew, son of Hachaliah and of a line of priests serving the God most high. The monarch had showered Nehemiah with honor, naming him his chief cupbearer in Susa—the fortress city that, with its pleasant fall and winter climate, had become a favorite of the Persian royalty.

To Nehemiah and his hand-selected corps of servants fell the task of securing the safety of Artaxerxes. It was an honor that included much more than merely tasting the king's wine before serving it as a precaution against poisoning by ever-ready rivals.

> *Nehemiah had earned the riches and position, watching over the king's life with his own and monitoring the royal family's table from harvest to preparation and serving.*

In choosing Nehemiah, Artaxerxes had included the Jew within a very small trusted circle of friends and counselors. Nehemiah had earned the riches and position, watching over the king's life with his own and monitoring the royal family's table from harvest to preparation and serving.

One day's conversation had robbed him of his happiness. A few months before, a delegation from Jerusalem, including his brother Hanani, had told him just how bad things had become in the Holy City: without protective walls and gates, it lay open to raids, its one-time glory gone in poverty and disgrace.

There had been days of tears, fasting, and prayers that saw sunrise and sunset. Nehemiah knew he had to risk approaching the king and asking him to reverse his earlier ruling. The cupbearer would risk all—friendship, position, perhaps even his life—by, in effect, telling the proud Artaxerxes he had been in error.

In the spring month of Nissan, 445 B.C., the time had come. Nehemiah's prayers and intellect had come up with a careful plan of approach to the king. There was no room for error—and that, most importantly, included having the direction and blessing of the Lord God of Abraham, Jacob, and Joseph.

And so Nehemiah prayed. It was a prayer for the ages. It was a prayer of honesty, openhearted confession, and no small measure of fear, buoyed by faith. How could he make the King of the universe remember His chastised people, know His servant's heart, and make Artaxerxes receptive to his plea?

In more detail this time, let's study that prayer's progression, a thought-by-thought model as sharp in focus as any laser today:

> O LORD, God of heaven, the great and awesome God, who keeps his covenant of love with those who love him and obey his commands.
> —NEHEMIAH 1:5

Nehemiah began by both honoring and identifying the one true Deity—and reminding Him of His special relationship with His chosen people.

Having established his acceptance of God's supreme place in the universe and His honor and purity as an eternal covenant-maker with His people,

Nehemiah then turned to the comparatively pitiful nature of those chosen ones. Time and time again he acknowledged that Israel had forgotten the commandments of God and spurned His love to the point where grace had to be balanced with divine judgment.

Israel had repeatedly fallen into the sins of its pagan neighbors, worshiping idols and even sacrificing their own children to demonic gods, making a mockery of God's love and authority.

No excuses came from the cupbearer. He even took personal responsibility for sin, including the sins of himself and his ancestors. "We deserve this," he said. Instead of lame explanations or personal denials, he bowed before his Creator, confessing his and his people's sin and accepting the punishment of exile as wholly just.

> Let your ear be attentive and your eyes open to hear the prayer your servant is praying before you day and night for your servants, the people of Israel. I confess the sins we Israelites, including myself and my father's house, have committed against you. We have acted very wickedly toward you. We have not

obeyed the commands, decrees and laws you
gave your servant Moses.

—NEHEMIAH 1:6–7

"Lord," Nehemiah was saying, "You warned us,
we sinned anyway, and we got what we deserved. We
accept that. And now, we embrace the promise You
gave us in Your love so long ago to Your servant and
our liberator from Egyptian slavery, Moses."

> Remember the instruction you gave your
> servant Moses, saying, "If you are unfaithful,
> I will scatter you among the nations, but if
> you return to me and obey my commands,
> then even if your exiled people are at the
> farthest horizon, I will gather them from
> there and bring them to the place I have
> chosen as a dwelling for my Name." They
> are your servants and your people, whom
> you redeemed by your great strength and
> your mighty hand.
>
> —NEHEMIAH 1:8–10

Does God need to be reminded of His promises?
Of course not. Nehemiah, in stating the provisions

made for national salvation from sin and heaven's wrath, was accepting both the promise and its responsibilities. The commitment, made through Moses so long ago at Mount Sinai, was being revived even as Nehemiah personally was revealing a tender, surrendered heart and spirit to his Maker.

It is a brief prayer, done in a minute or two. Humility. Confession. Acceptance. Grasping at the promise. Concluding in faith:

> O Lord, let your ear be attentive to the prayer of this your servant and to the prayer of your servants who delight in revering your name. Give your servant success today by granting him favor in the presence of this man.
>
> —NEHEMIAH 1:11

Nehemiah was now ready to approach Artaxerxes. Having completed his petition to the King of heaven, he walked toward the throne room of the man who held the power of life and death over the largest empire the world had ever known.

Nehemiah had probably begun life as a member of the extended royal family of Israel. However, along with other promising candidates for service to the triumphant Persian Empire, among his earliest memories would be those of a slave boy thrust into the society of the cruel, foreign despot Artaxerxes. Tempering this culture shock, though, were deep, strong roots in the faith of his Jewish fathers.

Nehemiah just didn't get up one day and have this magical prayer. He had been taught the principles behind it. Yes, Nehemiah, I'm sure, was raised in a fine Jewish home, and I'm sure he went to Sabbath school regularly. They taught him about the old Israelite kings, the heroes of their faith.

We all have heroes, men or women whose qualities earn them success against the odds. For me as a boy it was Vince Lombardi, who took a ragtag football team and turned them into the champion Green Bay Packers. Lombardi was a hero, as were his players, men like quarterback Bart Starr, receiver Max McGee, and linebacker Ray Nitschke. These were men we all wanted to be when we gathered for sandlot pickup games.

I knew Ray Nitschke well. In fact, it was one of the greatest blessings of my life to be used to lead the Packers' beloved number 66, the winner of two Super Bowls and member of the Pro Football Hall of Fame, to Christ. It began with one Sunday morning in 1994.

Ray's wife, Jackie, had recently recommitted her life to the Lord and was attending Bayside Church. I asked her that day how Ray was doing. "The golf course is his church on Sunday mornings," she told me. It was not a put-down; she regularly praised Ray for being a loving husband and great father.

Not long after that, Jackie invited Jan and me to a private box for a Packers game. Ray was gracious and friendly, but I learned that God and salvation were uncomfortable subjects for him. He had endured a tough childhood, losing both parents before entering high school.

An orphan at thirteen, he had gone to live with his older brother. He was adrift, the confusion and hurt from losing both parents at a young age leaving him skeptical about God's love and caring. After all, how could a loving God leave him without a mother and father at such a tender and critical age?

Sports became his purpose, and he excelled at high school, college, and professional levels alike. His generous nature and toughness were legendary and beloved by millions.

But in 1994, his glittering football career behind him, Ray Nitschke once more found a loved one in danger. Jackie had battled cancer for years, and at one point lay in a hospital bed in a coma. Joined by a visiting pastor and friend Dick Bernal, I went to pray for her.

Jackie awoke, a gleam on her face and the presence of God strong throughout the room; Ray too was visibly moved. She was released a few days later, on a Saturday. I dropped by to visit.

We prayed together again, and Ray followed me out into a hallway. He took me by the shoulders, hugged me, and planted a kiss on my cheek. "You're real," he said in his gruff voice. "I'm gonna come to your church." And he did, the next day, even though Jackie was still too weak to attend herself.

That morning, Ray Nitschke made his way to Bayside's altar and made a profession of Christ as his Lord and Savior. The golfing greens had lost a Sunday morning devotee, God had gained another son, and I had made a precious friend.

Jackie died in July 1996, and Ray mourned, but with the hope of reunion with his mate only Christ can give. On March 8, 1998, Ray himself died at age sixty-one of an apparent heart attack while visiting family and friends in Florida.

I preached at Ray's funeral in front of a packed auditorium at Bayside. Among the thousand or more attending were many of his former Green Bay team-mates, an NFL commissioner, and numerous public dignitaries. We closed the service with a final round of applause for Ray.

That service, broadcast live over Wisconsin television, was viewed by many thousands more. But along with a memorial to Ray, they also heard his testimony and learned how one of football's most feared line-backers had turned his heart over to Christ.

That service was also something of a turning point for Bayside. A number of those grizzled foot-ball veterans and others who heard that message later accepted Christ, and the association of our church with such a beloved sports figure brought many more people through our doors.

GOD'S FAVOR

The young Nehemiah had such heroes, too. He had surely heard the story of his people's patriarch Joseph and how he too had received God's favor through godly preparation and integrity. Joseph could well have been little Nehemiah's hero. And as a captive slave boy at the mercy of a foreign king, he likely identified with the example of unswerving obedience and favor Joseph's life represented.

Reading Genesis 39:3–4, Nehemiah would have learned how Joseph responded to being thrown into a pit by his jealous brothers and then sold into slavery to a caravan headed for Egypt. Bought by Potiphar, a captain of Pharaoh's guard, Joseph could have been despondent and sullen, vowing revenge. Instead, he chose a path of honoring the right and of serving with integrity.

The verses read: "When his master saw that the LORD was with him and that the LORD gave him success in everything he did, Joseph found favor in his eyes and became his attendant."

The Lord was with him. All he did prospered, and Potiphar took notice. Joseph had been kidnapped, betrayed, and sold as a slave by his own flesh and blood; yet here he was, so trusted by this Egyptian government official that he was given charge of everything Potiphar had. Potiphar left all his affairs to Joseph, even to the point he didn't even know what was in his own pocketbook.

Potiphar had it made, as Genesis 39:6 tells us: "He left in Joseph's care everything he had; with Joseph in charge, he did not concern himself with anything except the food he ate."

But blessings from God on her husband's estate, the wealth rolling in from Potiphar's fields, and growing investments watched over by this extraordinarily talented Hebrew slave were not enough for one particularly desperate housewife. Mrs. Potiphar, Genesis 39:6–7 tells us, had designs on the "well-built and handsome" Joseph.

It would have been so easy for Joseph to give in. Potiphar had trusted him with everything in his household, including the welfare of his family. But he said no, and he did more than that. When Mrs. Potiphar, bedroom eyes alight, caught him alone in the house and grabbed him by the cloak, Joseph shed the garment and literally ran away from sin.

> *Joseph had been kidnapped, betrayed, and sold as a slave by his own flesh and blood; yet here he was, so trusted by this Egyptian government official that he was given charge of everything Potiphar had.*

The woman of the house now had some explaining to do. But it was her word against Joseph's, and she had his cloak. Attempted rape, she told Potiphar. He believed her and had Joseph thrown into prison.

But really, it was Joseph's integrity that landed him in Pharaoh's maximum security prison, a place where the kingdom's special enemies languished as they awaited punishment, often execution. Sometimes doing what is right comes with a painful price.

What had not changed, though, was God's favor—the assigned advantage—to His servant. In a short time, the warden also saw that there was something special about this particular inmate. Joseph won favor behind bars, too, and soon the warden delegated prison operations to Joseph.

Soon, Joseph was meeting out-of-favor members of Pharaoh's court. As a boy tending his father Jacob's flocks, Joseph had dreamed prophecies; now Pharaoh's cupbearer and baker had experienced troubling dreams and Joseph interpreted them. It was bad news for the baker, who was executed three days later, just as the Hebrew slave had said. But the cupbearer, also as Joseph foretold, was restored to his duties.

Later, when Pharaoh himself was troubled by dreams, the cupbearer recommended Joseph to do what the ruler's own fortune-tellers could not— explain the meaning of the nocturnal visions of cows and wheat. "Seven years of bumper crops followed by seven years of famine," Joseph told him, crediting God for the answers.

Joseph advised the Egyptian king to prepare, storing away grain against the time of crop failures and hunger to come. "Great idea," Pharaoh probably nodded to himself. "None of my counselors and soothsayers could figure this out, but here comes this Hebrew slave.... *Hmm.*" And he decided:

> Since God has made all this known to you, there is no one so discerning and wise as you. You shall be in charge.... Only with respect to the throne will I be greater than you.
>
> —GENESIS 41:39

Favor can be the ticket to some pretty wild rides, but the outcome is in the hands of God. I like to say that Joseph had been *pitted, potted,* and *putted.* He was tossed in a pit and sold as a slave by his brothers, sold to Potiphar and imprisoned, and then put in charge of a powerful kingdom.

> *Integrity of heart and action are ongoing commitments—matters of daily choices.*

What better role model for Nehemiah than Joseph—the life of another young Jewish exile in dire circumstances who rose to do great things for his people because he had the unassailable favor of God? This assigned advantage nothing on Earth could defeat.

Because of Joseph's faith, Nehemiah had a hero to emulate. And today, because of Nehemiah's courage to follow that example, we have him and his simple, powerful prayer to help light us to our own paths to favor from our Lord.

But to follow any path, you must walk. Those steps come with living a godly life and applying His Word to our decisions and priorities. We live and work in difficult environments—the office, the classroom, and the factory all have their demands and pressure to compromise. Like Joseph and Nehemiah, we must resolve to stay true to what is right, good, and holy.

Integrity of heart and action are ongoing commitments; they are matters of daily choices. So pray for favor.

Live like you expect it, but make decisions God can honor. If you apply the principles we explore together in this little book, you too may be called to do great things—in your family, your church, your community, your nation, your world—and all of that with the obstacle-clearing, miraculous favor of God.

Chapter 3

FIRST, YOU PRAY

*Dialogue with God begins with
discipline.*

O N THE EVENING news, in magazine and newspaper articles, from the pulpit, and even from worried doctors during that annual physical examination, we have been told time and time again that our lives have become just too busy.

And the statistics support the conclusions. Since 1950, according to a Center for Popular Economics article, Americans' free time has steadily deteriorated. We now work nearly two hundred hours more each year than other civilized nations, taking just thirteen days annual vacation on average, compared to four to five weeks required among western European countries.[1]

What about "quality time" at home with spouses and children? The U.S. Bureau of Labor Statistics found that in 2004, Americans working full-time jobs could expect to have three hours of leisure time out of their days;[2] this is not much time when you also have a family to consider and hopefully nurture.

These facts have not given us pause, nor have they stirred a commitment to reevaluate our priorities. Instead, we have turned to technology to find ways to do more in less time. Minicomputers, or PDAs (personal digital assistants), are slipped into our pockets to give us instant access to schedules and contact lists.

More recently, these gadgets have been combined with "smart phones," cellular handsets that strap to our hips like an Old West revolver. Instead of shooting rattlesnakes or highwaymen, though, we use the little marvels of circuitry to "shoot" each other text messages, pictures, and calls. The latest of these gadgets even allows the owner to watch television-like news, sports, and music clips.

Ah. Just what we need, right? More quality time with our electronics. And yet, these gadgets have become almost invaluable in our hectic personal and professional lives.

> *A prayer life is essential for claiming God's favor, and discipline is critical to create that quiet place inside where we dedicate time each day to pray and to listen.*

When I was pastor at Bayside Church, my computer would signal me when an appointment was coming, pulling up the information on who, when, and why. Just another personal example of how we have squeezed every minute—every second—out of our days to be productive, to keep up with demands on our time.

But God doesn't own a PDA, a smart phone, or a computer. Instead, He calls on our spirits in a "still small voice," as 1 Kings 19:12 (KJV) tells us. It is a voice to be listened for, and unless our spiritual ears are cupped and intently focused to His words, our quality time with God can get lost in the mayhem of daily life.

A prayer life is essential for claiming God's favor, and discipline is critical to create that quiet place inside where we dedicate time each day to pray and to listen.

God yearns for a dialogue with His children, and He wants the opportunity to build our understanding of His ways, to build our trust in Him, and to shape lumps of willing, spiritual clay into vessels into which He can pour His favor, His assigned advantage.

So, come on. If we can type in our daily appointments, prioritize our tasks, and keep track of new addresses, telephone numbers, e-mails, birthdays, anniversaries, and so on, why can't we make a daily appointment to pray?

Jot it down, and there it is, a commitment made. The time is set aside; the task is assigned top, "A-1" priority, and you have set it up to repeat every day.

That's pretty much what Nehemiah did, though I doubt there were day planners on clay tablets or sheepskins back then. But he made that commitment, and it is clear that prayer and his devotion to God were number one every day. That's how he could plead with confidence, "O Lord! Let your ear be attentive," and have the expectation that his God would do exactly that.

Nehemiah had discovered what many of us are beginning to experience again today: a pattern of prayer. Think of it; your first prayer likely was a pattern: "Now I lay me down to sleep. I pray the Lord my soul to keep...." And as a young adult Christian, the pattern may have been responsive or congregational and in the form of the Lord's Prayer: "Our Father, which art in heaven, Hallowed be thy name. Thy kingdom come. Thy will be done..." (Matt. 6:9–10, KJV).

> *A bold and godly prayer life will always build positive things to advance the kingdom of heaven.*

I have incorporated many prayer patterns into my life, and I learned some of them while serving several years on the board of Dr. David Yonggi Cho's ministry. Do you think this pastor built the 800,000-strong Yoido Full Gospel Church in Seoul, South Korea, without prayer? Prayer was and remains the foundation stone for what Dr. Cho and God's favor built into the world's largest single church.

Dr. Cho taught me many different prayers, and to those have come others, each in their time and all worth incorporating into my time with God. Variety is the spice of life, the saying goes, and it holds true in your conversations with God, too.

These patterns have ranged from the eloquent, profound, and beautiful "Jesus prayer" of John 17:1–26 (KJV), "Father, the hour is come; glorify thy Son, that thy Son also may glorify thee," to the more recent petition of the blessed life in miniature in the prayer of Jabez—two verses that shine like diamonds in a field of rocks, right in the middle of one of the most monotonous genealogical recitations of the Old Testament.

> And Jabez was more honourable than his brethren....And [he] called on the God of Israel, saying, Oh that thou wouldest bless me indeed, and enlarge my coast, and that thine hand might be with me, and that thou wouldest keep me from evil, that it may not grieve me! And God granted him that which he requested.
>
> —1 CHRONICLES 4:9–10, KJV

That's it. Yet Bruce Wilkinson, the internationally renowned founder of Walk Thru the Bible Ministries, has prayed that brief, direct petition to the Lord most of his life. In 2000, he even wrote a runaway best seller entitled *The Prayer of Jabez*.

It is another simple and honest prayer that God listened to and granted, because the petitioner was a man of honor, like Nehemiah. The Lord favors integrity. A bold and godly prayer life will always build positive things to advance the kingdom of heaven.

Of course, Nehemiah did not need to plow through ancient genealogies to learn how to pray, though as a devoted student of Scripture, he certainly knew of Jabez. The young Jewish captive, being groomed for service in the Persian royal court, probably lionized Joseph and his Egyptian sojourn of faith, too.

But Nehemiah did not have to look that far back for an example, either. Indeed, he had an older contemporary to model: Ezra.

Here was another man of integrity, purpose, and prayer. At a critical time, this scribe was the catalyst to win then King Darius's approval to rebuild the Jewish temple. Ezra also was a spiritual leader, helping the remnant of Jews freed to rebuild Solomon's monument to God to also rediscover His laws.

The callings of Ezra and Nehemiah, though nearly two decades apart, overlapped in the broader scope of God's purpose. Their missions even complemented each other. Together, their favor with God and the monarchy had seen the temple rise in Jerusalem once more.

In Ezra's own account of the return of Jewish settlers to rebuild the temple in Jerusalem, he frankly told not only of God's interventions on behalf of His people—but also of the continuing counterstrokes the enemy took to stall or, if possible, to thwart the project.

One technique proved especially effective: the smear campaign. It was a diabolical recipe: Mix equal parts lies and innuendo, add a hefty measure of greed, dash in the yeast of fear that comes from having an uncertain and distant throne, and bake into a letter frosted with the sweet, fawning words of corrupt bureaucrats.

Artaxerxes swallowed it whole, and you can see why as you read it.

> The king should know that the Jews who came up to us from you have gone to Jerusalem and are rebuilding that rebellious and wicked city. They are restoring the walls and repairing the foundations. Furthermore, the king should know that if this city is built and its walls are restored, no more taxes, tribute or duty will be paid, and the royal revenues will suffer. Now since we are under obligation to the palace and it is not proper

for us to see the king dishonored, we are sending this message to inform the king, so that a search may be made in the archives of your predecessors. In these records you will find that this city is a rebellious city, troublesome to kings and provinces, a place of rebellion from ancient times. That is why this city was destroyed. We inform the king that if this city is built and its walls are restored, you will be left with nothing in Trans-Euphrates.

—EZRA 4:12–16

Rebellious in the past and inclined to be so again...*hmm.* A temple is one thing, but strong walls to withstand an army—perhaps *his* army? And no more taxes or tribute? Now, wait a minute!

So Artaxerxes had his court historians check out this distant province of Judah and its capital, Jerusalem. "This city has a long history of revolt against kings and has been a place of rebellion and sedition," they concluded.

Artaxerxes summoned his secretary and dashed off a reply: "Stop all work until you hear from me again!" The king had set himself squarely against rebuilding the city; all work was at a standstill.

How many times have you started something you thought was good and right, only to come up against a roadblock? We all have come to that point, and yet if God is in it, you cannot just give up. Don't walk away; things can change.

Ezra and the Jews in Jerusalem were stymied. But in the fortress city of Susa, God moved the heart of Nehemiah, and that was the beginning of new hope.

> When I heard these things, I sat down and wept. For some days I mourned and fasted and prayed before the God of heaven.
> —NEHEMIAH 1:4

Nehemiah mourned for the devastated Jerusalem, the once-shining City of David, sprawling wall-less and helpless around its rebuilt temple. For his brothers and sisters eking out a living in the rubble, stalked by hunger and poverty and fearful of attack, he fasted.

And when his eyes were red and swollen, his unfed body exhausted by the grief and anger and despair,

Nehemiah prayed from a broken, surrendered, and humbled heart.

What things are causing you to pray with such integrity of spirit today? Is it a lost loved one, perhaps that child, sibling, or parent who walks alone, ignoring God's love and salvation gift?

Do scenes of war, political unrest, and natural disasters propel you to your knees? Who could not be moved by scenes of the ruin and death left by earthquakes, tsunamis, and terrorist suicide bombings that fill our news seemingly every day?

> *We all have come up against roadblocks, but don't walk away; things can change.*

Or is it more personal, perhaps the frustration and even self-loathing that can build with persistent lack of success? What area of your life, what failure continues to rob you of joy and peace? What lack of confidence keeps you from stepping out in faith?

What will it take to bring you to your knees? Let

me tell you the story of a troubled couple that God led me to minister to through what would seem an incredible and horrible set of circumstances. I know today, and so do they, that what happened was nothing but the miraculous healing ministry of Christ.

I met Tom, John, and Susan while out one day driving. (At their request, we will not use their real names; secondary details of their story have also been altered.) I had stopped at an area business and struck up a conversation with Tom, one of the customers there. I ended up sharing Christ with him as we stood there in the store.

Perhaps you just blinked there. But yes, it's true—I always try to find a way to share Jesus with people I meet; it becomes second nature.

But let me continue with the story. Sometime after I'd left the store, I got a call from Tom, asking to meet with me. He was desperate, and I soon learned why: He was involved in an affair with a married woman, Susan. Tom, who also was married, was living in fear. He feared Susan's husband, John, and thought that John might resort to violence to settle the score.

Somehow the three of them all managed to meet with me in my office. There was a lot of anger, threats of violence, and confusion. But John, Susan, and Tom wanted their own marriages to work. I told them that this thing was so sordid that they must give their lives to Christ. And they did.

Through counseling, prayer, and a lot of forgiveness, John and Susan's marriage was restored, and although Tom's marriage did not survive that affair, I am happy to say that he has continued his walk with Christ.

But the story isn't over. This was just the beginning. John and Susan have become mentors for couples in stressed marriages. They have seen God work dramatic miracles in couples whose marriages were to be final within days. They have also led many of their friends and family to Christ.

How did this all start? Simply by sharing the Lord with a fellow customer. One person, in dire circumstances, ready for Christ, became a spiritual domino that resulted in many more souls enlisting in the kingdom of God.

Are you finally able to pray for a vision larger than yourself? Then you need to have the heart of Nehemiah and have the pattern of his prayer on your lips.

What was the heart of Nehemiah's prayer? He wanted favor with God and the king. Nehemiah could simply have prayed, "God, help me rebuild the wall," or "God, let King Artaxerxes give me time off so I can go to Jerusalem."

> *When you are living right and desire*
> *God's blessings for you to undertake*
> *a vision He gave you, God will bless*
> *you with His favor in your home,*
> *your neighborhood, your church, your*
> *workplace, your life.*

Either of those prayers might have been all right; they were specific and focused on the goal. But Nehemiah wanted something more, an assurance beyond an aristocratic nod that might again be changed by the political winds. He wanted Artaxerxes' favor—

that special, unassailable, assigned advantage from the king.

And Nehemiah knew that sort of blessing would not easily come from the scepter of his Persian master. Yes, Nehemiah was Artaxerxes' cupbearer and had earned his trust. But bottom line, no one was forgetting the social and political gulf that yawned between the king and the man who was his slave, no matter how glorified.

Nehemiah knew that before he could hope for the favor of the king, he had to have an assigned advantage from the King of kings and Lord of lords. Nehemiah 5:19 puts it this way: "Remember me with favor, O my God, for all I have done for these people."

When you are living right, when you have the desire for God's blessings in order for you to undertake a vision He gave you, God will bless you with His favor in your home, your neighborhood, your church, your workplace, your life.

Nehemiah was about to discover that. As we continue on this journey with him, so will you.

Chapter 4

PARTNERSHIP—
A VISION IN COMMON

Booker T. Washington got it. Will you?

 O FIND AN example of a Nehemiah-like hero in our own nation's history, consider Booker T. Washington. Like Nehemiah, Washington was born into slavery; like his Jewish predecessor, this African American spent his formative years as a servant in the society ruled by his oppressors; and like Nehemiah, Washington was a man of uncommon intellect.

In his autobiography, *Up From Slavery*, Washington talks about humble, even cruel, beginnings. Born in 1856, just prior to the outbreak of the Civil War, his father was apparently a white man from a neighboring Virginia plantation who never showed interest in his welfare or that of his mother; she would cook for their masters and then curl up for the night with her son on the dirt floor of their small, one-room slave cabin.

> *"Character, not circumstances, makes the man. I will permit no man to narrow or degrade my soul by making me hate him."* —*Booker T. Washington*

The North's victory over the slave-holding South set Washington and his mother free. In search of a new life, they settled in the salt-mining town of Malden, West Virginia. The boy was soon packing salt with his stepfather, but he had a dream: he wanted to read. It began with a tattered copy of a beginner's alphabet and spelling book, and when a makeshift school for black children was opened, Booker T. Washington was primed and ready to begin a lifetime of education.

As he grew, Washington learned, devouring books after long days processing salt and later mining coal. Also growing was his faith, one that began early with forgiveness of his former owners and the racism he encountered throughout his life. His faith also taught him principles he would share with generations of African Americans to come.

Washington wrote, "Every persecuted individual and race should get much consolation out of the great human law, which is universal and eternal, that merit, no matter under what skin found, is, in the long run, recognized and rewarded."[1]

This truly American hero would go on from the soot and sweat of labor in the depths of the earth to take a spotty education overcome by a brilliant mind to graduate from what is now Hampton University and then to study at Wayland Seminary. By 1879, all of twenty-three years old, Washington was teaching industrial arts to fellow blacks at night school; he did so well that Washington won the admiration of his white benefactor and became the founding president of what today is Alabama's Tuskegee University.

Washington taught self-reliance to his students, and they built much of the growing Tuskegee campus, learning engineering and trades as they did. When he died in 1915, he was a renowned educator, popular speaker, and author of numerous books. And in a final act of irony and honor, the plantation where the slave-turned-hero was born is today a national monument.

Like Nehemiah, the importance of character was paramount in the gaining of favor from both oppressors and his own people for Booker T. Washington. He repeatedly wrote and spoke about the priority of principle: "Character, not circumstances, makes the man,"[2] he said, and in an attitude that put feet to his faith, he also said, "I will permit no man to narrow and degrade my soul by making me hate him."[3]

In his January 2007 *Leadership Wired* newsletter, inspirational author John C. Maxwell could have been expanding on another Washington quote, "Leadership is character," when he connected that principle to the very foundation of becoming the kind of godly servant people will follow:

Choose today the legacy you want to leave others. People will summarize your life in one sentence—pick it now! Don't make your friends and family guess at your life's purpose at your funeral....When you consistently combine character with competence, you establish credibility.[4]

Character. Integrity. Favor. Those are the ingredients for effective leadership and godly service alike. It applies to the individual, ready to be called by God to great things, and it is imperative for the church body that seeks and is gifted with that same assigned advantage in an inspired partnership with its spiritual leaders.

> *Character is paramount in*
> *the gaining of favor.*

Do you want the favor of God on your life? Live a life that is solid on principle and full in reflecting the character of the Word of God taken into your mind and heart. And as your character grows more

Christlike in obedience to the Lord and application of godly principles, so will integrity—and your horizons.

> *Character. Integrity. Favor. Those are the ingredients for effective leadership and godly service alike.*

It is the same for a congregation committed to exercising the favor factor. Apply the principles, and the favor of God will come upon your church and its people. Your church will become a lighthouse of deep character, a beacon of right choices and motives.

Nehemiah's calling was to rebuild Jerusalem's walls. Long before he did that, though, he had honed his management skills, his character, and his reputation as a slave to a wicked king. God's favor, and that of Artaxerxes, put a young man in the trusted role of cupbearer, and that became a partnership that led to a change of the royal heart.

Nehemiah's partnership extended beyond the court in Susa; he knew he had to build it among the discouraged and defeated Jews of Jerusalem, too.

Nehemiah's position of favor put him on the road to Judah, escorted by a small army with letters of authority and a fortune with which to buy the supplies and materials needed to restore the walls and respect of the City of David. During the weeks it likely took to cover the caravan routes to his long ago home province, Nehemiah was praying, planning, and polishing his strategy for enlisting his brothers in the cause.

He now needed a new partnership, one that would require many to adopt the vision of this emissary from the king. He needed the trust of a people downtrodden and distrustful of the intentions of a distant monarch.

All successes in life require a guiding motivation. Think of those things that commonly drive men to long hours and sacrifice: money, recognition, and honor; providing for one's family; preparing a carefree retirement.

But Nehemiah's motive? Return with me for a moment to Nehemiah 1:3–4. He learns his people are "in great trouble and disgrace." The walls of the city are broken down, its once-sturdy gates reduced to charred embers. "I sat down and wept...mourned and fasted and prayed before the God of heaven," Nehemiah said.

He knew too that his people's very existence as God's chosen nation teetered on history's precipice. Jerusalem's condition was a reflection of the condition of captive Israel's heart.

Nehemiah was also aware that the longer his people stayed within the cities of their captors, more of his brothers and sisters would turn to the idols and pagan religions flourishing in the multicultural realm of Artaxerxes.

The same God works within the hearts and passions of His people today. All those who call upon the name of the Lord are entitled to choose the blessings of a life of favor, to reap the fruits of integrity and faithful preparation, and to build spiritual partnerships fueled by the assigned advantage of heaven.

> As God's fellow workers we urge you not
> to receive God's grace in vain. For he says,

"In the time of my favor I heard you, and
in the day of salvation I helped you." I tell
you, now is the time of God's favor, now is
the time of salvation.

—2 CORINTHIANS 6:1–2

New Testament or Old Testament, the favor
factor echoes through time. Isaiah 49:8–9 says:

In the time of my favor I will answer you,
    and in the day of salvation I will help you;
I will keep you and will make you
    to be a covenant for the people,
to restore the land
    and to reassign its desolate inheritances,
to say to the captives, "Come out,"
    and to those in darkness, "Be free!"

The passage concludes: "They will feed beside the
roads and find pasture on every barren hill." Now
there's a promise.

Remember we discussed earlier the importance
of attitude in seeing the favor factor in effect in the
workplace?

> *It is from a forgiving and forgiven heart, and an obedient spirit, that the favor factor is born.*

But the job, important to our welfare as it is, is but one small part of life. And in a Christian's life, having a heart for the lost—on the job, in the classroom, for the neighbors next door and down the street—puts you on your knees with a broken heart.

Then you can pray Nehemiah's prayer, the prayer of Jabez, and, with humble confidence, the traditional Lord's Prayer of Matthew 6:9–13. You probably know it; now read it aloud. See, hear, and absorb the words as if coming for the first time from the lips of Jesus:

> Our Father in heaven,
> hallowed be your name,
> your kingdom come,
> your will be done
>   on earth as it is in heaven.
> Give us today our daily bread.
> Forgive us our debts,
>   as we also have forgiven our debtors.

And lead us not into temptation,
but deliver us from the evil one.

Jesus underscored the importance of forgiveness given and received. "For if you forgive men when they sin against you, your heavenly Father will also forgive you," He said (v. 14).

It is from that kind of heart, and for that sort of obedient spirit, that the favor factor is born. And from that attitude and vision flows the ability to generate teamwork that will be blessed with God's assigned advantage over any foe it faces.

Let's look at team building, Nehemiah style, as recounted in the second chapter of his book, verses 11–18. First off, he didn't rush to get things going before he saw for himself how things were. After three days, he set out in the dark of night with a few chosen men; he hadn't told anyone there what his mission was.

Nehemiah did a complete survey of the city's broken-down walls and gateways, and when he was satisfied he had complete knowledge of the scope of the project, he began recruiting.

> You see the trouble we are in: Jerusalem
> lies in ruins, and its gates have been burned
> with fire. Come, let us rebuild the wall
> of Jerusalem, and we will no longer be in
> disgrace.
>
> —NEHEMIAH 2:17

Notice Nehemiah had chosen the time and place to spring his plan and to maximize the support he could gather from the city's residents. What did they likely see? This brother of theirs arriving with a king's guard, treasure, building supplies, and work orders from Artaxerxes himself.

They also would notice the confidence of this fellow Nehemiah. He had a plan—and the materials, political support, and funding to make it happen. All they had to do was sign on to make Nehemiah's mission their own.

"Let us start rebuilding," they tell Nehemiah. They saw God's favor and wanted to be part of that. Hope had arrived; now was the time. "Let's do it!" might be the response today.

The people were behind it. Now Nehemiah's army of rebuilding needed its generals, sergeants, and foot soldiers—the people to implement an organization, to divide a massive project into phases, and to make sure one section of wall would meet another and all sections would be of the same design and quality. Below are four things Nehemiah did to accomplish this.

1. Turned to the priesthood

First, Nehemiah wisely turned to a trusted local authority figure within the one group of Jews commanding respect: the priesthood. By working with and connecting to the chief priest, Eliashib, the entire priesthood rallied to the cause, giving it a proper beginning.

2. Dedicated the work to God

That brings the second highlight of Nehemiah's team-building strategy: dedicate the work to God.

> Eliashib the high priest and his fellow priests went to work and rebuilt the Sheep Gate. They dedicated it and set its doors in place, building as far as the Tower of the Hundred, which they dedicated, and as far as the Tower of Hananel.
>
> —NEHEMIAH 3:1

3. Worked as brothers

Next, the third phase of Nehemiah's organizational plan: work as brothers. That is exactly what unfolded as the wall slowly rose again. Each group of Jews would complete its section and join it to the next.

Read about it in Nehemiah 3:3–5. The sons of Hassenaah built the Fish Gate, carefully crafting its beams, bolts, and bars to fit into the next section, one erected by Meremoth, the son of Uriah. Next to him was Meshullam, the son of Berekiah, and then further down the wall was Zadok, son of Baana—and so on; everyone working together.

4. Remembered that God's work creates true heroes

Number four in Nehemiah's team-building paradigm: remembering God's work creates true heroes. Nehemiah names them, the workers who rebuild, even as he carefully honors the memories of King David and his family as he and his crews make repairs to safeguard their tombs.

It is important to remember the lives of the heroes of our faith, to honor their commitment to God, and to emulate their examples in winning our own portions of heavenly favor.

It was, and remains, all about the kingdom of God. His forgiveness is our passport; His blessings are the results of applying the principles of the gospel. We do that individually, and we must do that as a body of believers.

What is your calling—your part in the kingdom-building project all Christians are called on to labor for? Maybe it is targeting and praying for neighbors, or being the best mom or dad or best employee you can be. God will open the windows of heaven on you if you do it His way.

Favor comes in many forms: a happy family and children accepting Christ and growing into adults you can be proud of. Or it might be that when you walk into a room, the whispers are about the divine charisma you emanate. There is something about you that, at some point, gives you an audience and a chance to share Christ.

What is perhaps the most difficult of Nehemiah's team-building plan to implement? I believe it is in accepting authority. Bottom line: you must respect your leader.

Oh, it can be hard to submit and work with authority figures. But believe me, if you have a problem with it, so will your children—and with you. God moves through authority figures, and a lot of Christians are finding the favor of God elusive because they have not incorporated this into their lives.

Do you come home from work and complain about how bad the boss is, how inept he or she is? Are your children listening? You are playing into the hands of the enemy—you will not have God's favor.

Instead, why not get to the job early and pray over the office or work site and all those who will labor there that day, including your manager or employer? A lot of bosses are frustrated, unhappy people under pressure and without a relationship with God to face it. We need to be praying for them and modeling Christ to them, not undercutting and backbiting.

I challenge you to dedicate that portion of the wall where you work to the kingdom of God. Seek out other believers to do the same, and see if the atmosphere and productivity don't change dramatically for the better.

> *God moves through authority figures, and a lot of Christians are finding the favor of God elusive because they have not incorporated this into their lives.*

It is never too late to start on the road to favor. It always begins with obedience to God's principles, as my friend, Minneapolis television sports reporter Ryan Kibbe, will tell you.

Like many of us, Ryan grew up in a Christian home, but then a crisis came along that broke down both family and faith. In Ryan's case, it was the divorce of his Southern Baptist minister parents when he was fourteen. By seventeen, angry and hurt, he was turning to alcohol; his relationship with his parents, especially his father and new stepmother, was seemingly broken beyond healing.

"I blamed them all for ruining my life, and I took it out on them and other people. I lived victimized.

I trusted no one and took no personal responsibility for my actions," he recalls. "I began to feel that God abandoned me, so I abandoned Him."

By twenty-four, Ryan was a full-blown alcoholic. The booze took its toll on his professional life, too, costing him two jobs in the broadcast news industry. He was spiraling out of control. Ironically, it was his father who intervened, driving to Iowa and back to Texas to get his troubled son into a twelve-step recovery program.

A time of painful introspection ensued. As Ryan puts it, "My onion began to peel." At the ragged, bleeding core of it all was this conviction: if I am not a somebody, then I must be a nobody.

He had taken his last drink on July 2, 1996. Four years later, enduring many "white-knuckle" moments and numerous Alcoholics Anonymous meetings, Ryan was still sober. He was also miserable, fighting a new addiction to gambling and working at a Green Bay, Wisconsin, TV station.

He admits that loneliness and feelings of despair led him to visit Bayside Church on a Sunday in April 2001. The next day, he showed up at the church office, asking for someone to talk to. One of our seasoned Christian men took Ryan on for one-on-one discipleship, listening to his heart and gradually, steadily leading him to a new relationship with Christ.

One of the teachings of our church is the blessings the Lord gives to those who honor giving. We believe tithing is a principle of obedience that God honors through all aspects of a believer's life. When Ryan learned of this, he decided to obey.

"I settled in my heart to do it, all or nothing. I dove in headfirst, and within those first three months, God overwhelmed me with blessings. His presence cured my loneliness, I got a substantial pay raise, I made new friends, and on July 4, 2001, I met my future wife," Ryan recounts.

> *"I never experienced the fullness of His 'assigned advantage' until I stepped out in faith and obeyed."*

In the next four years, his income doubled, and his professional opportunities grew, along with the esteem of his superiors and colleagues. In 2002, Ryan was honored with the Edward R. Murrow Award for sports reporting.[5] The winning segment was about the role of faith within the Green Bay Packers football team following the 9/11 terrorist attacks.

In July 2005, he moved to a larger TV market in Minneapolis, another big raise, and a work schedule that allowed him to have weekends off with his growing family.

He also learned that in addition to giving from his checkbook, he needed to give of himself. Along with his wife, Hope, he began working in the church's children's and youth programs; later, he began participating in personal evangelism, taking his testimony to the streets along with other Christians, praying for hundreds of willing strangers.

And what of his relationship with his father, mother, and stepmother? Forgiveness and reconciliation have come over the years.

"God's blessings and favor have been with me since the day I got saved," Ryan says now. "Yet I never experienced the fullness of His 'assigned advantage' until I stepped out in faith and obeyed [the call to share Christ's love]."

Chapter 5

PLANNING FOR FAVOR

When success comes, do you know your first step?

ON THE DAY Nehemiah prayed for God's favor, he was ready for the consequences of "yes."

That was no small thing. Consider this: if the Persian Empire of Artaxerxes' time had something like a Las Vegas—and human nature being what it always has been, it probably had an equivalent—the odds laid on wagers over a positive outcome for Nehemiah's appointment with the king would have been astronomically long.

Artaxerxes, the conqueror of the known world's great civilizations, reversing his own edict against the rebuilding of Jerusalem? This self-described favorite of the Zoroastrian religion's creator god, Ahura Mazda, admitting he had been wrong? That would have been the epitome of a "sucker's bet."

In other words, Nehemiah would need a miracle. But he knew where miracles came from and for whom they were granted: servants whose lives warranted the ear of the almighty Lord of heaven and Earth.

How long did Nehemiah pray? Many hours, days, weeks, and even months were spent fasting, weeping, and repeating the petition of a spirit humbled and broken before God.

"O Lord, let your ear be attentive to the prayer of this your servant and to the prayer of your servants who delight in revering your name." In other words, Nehemiah is crying, "God, LISTEN TO ME!" And he follows that with his spiritual credentials—words as much for Nehemiah's ears and confidence before God as they were for Him who had known and directed the life of this captive Israelite from his very conception in the womb.

"Give your servant success today by granting him favor in the presence of this man."

How many times have we replied, "I'm waiting on the Lord," when asked how a prayer request is faring? When the answer comes, then what? Are we prepared to implement the blessing immediately, or are we so stunned God said yes that we are paralyzed, perhaps as opportunity begins to fade?

> *Nehemiah did things God's way, and that example changed an entire kingdom.*

Nehemiah planned for yes. During that period of fasting and prayer, he also was thinking, "What needs to be done if Artaxerxes grants me favor? What will I do with the king's assigned advantage?"

We discussed earlier in this book what an honor—and heavy responsibility—being a cupbearer to the king was. Surely God's hand was on Nehemiah to rise so far within the royal court. But the Lord also had blessed this young refugee with a fine mind and the gift for organization; he stood out by performance and excellence.

In Nehemiah, we find a young man who applied God's principles; he lived a godly life and earned a reputation for integrity and management of men and resources put under him. He did things God's way, and that example changed an entire kingdom.

It was the favor of God, not so much some great miracle or a sign. Now, I love miracles, to see God doing marvelous things, but that was not the case here so much as it was the result of a young man applying God's principles.

As a young man I spent a summer working with a surveyor. To be effective in plotting out property lines and easements, you have to check back to the point where you know the variables all were right. You look through the surveyor's scope or "shoot back" and "turn the angles" to find that previous fixed point. That's how surveyors find and confirm directions.

It's the same idea with living a life by godly principles that will keep you in line with God's favor. In our spiritual surveying, we have many examples to follow—Moses, David, Joseph, Nehemiah, and others—all of them connecting with tried-and-true principles that all point to our "fixed point," our Lord and God.

As a new Christian working for a leading farm equipment company in Racine, Wisconsin, I learned firsthand how God's favor hovers over our intentions and deeds.

The job, as a technical clerk, was rewriting change orders on parts for tractors. Mind you, this was in the precomputer days, but it wasn't rocket science, and it took me about a week to figure it out. After a while, I was able to get the work down to about four hours a day—and no Saturdays. Some there wanted me to slow down, to not set such a pace, to not, in effect, raise management's expectations. Instead, I asked the boss for more to do in order to stay productive and to be the kind of employee I thought would honor Christ.

My idea was that, "I'm now representing Jesus Christ! I'm not going to just sit around, and I'm not going to milk this job, no matter what others say." And God would honor that.

Carl Pavia, the father of my future wife, Jan, worked there, too. He was greatly respected for his work ethic and wisdom. Over the years, the bosses had learned to listen to him and count on his integrity.

In short order, the Lord called me into the ministry, and Jan and I became engaged. I knew I needed to attend Bible college to prepare, but my employers had been so good to me I was not entirely sure how to break the news to them that I had to leave.

So, I asked Carl. He thought it over for a while and then told me, "Go in and tell them you're getting married soon, been working hard, etc., and ask them for a ridiculous raise. Then when they turn you down, you'll be free to go."

It sounded good to me. But I didn't want to take any chances. Instead of asking for 10 or 20 percent or something like that, I went into the boss's office and asked for double my pay. To my surprise, the boss didn't immediately throw me out. "Let me talk about this with the people upstairs," he said.

A few hours later I was called into the office, prepared for the expected refusal and then my easy transition to giving notice. I braced myself as the boss began to speak, and then I struggled to keep my jaw from dropping to the floor.

Instead of rejection, he told me how much the company had appreciated my hard work, my willingness to take on more than the job called for, and how they didn't want to lose me. "You've got your raise, Arni," he said.

Oh, boy. Well, so much for the best-laid plans of Carl and Arni. I then spilled the beans, telling the boss how I'd expected to be turned down, thought that would make it easier on everyone...but I was being called into the ministry and would have to leave, regardless.

We ended that day in some laughter and friendship. Instead of disappointment, I left good feelings behind when I went on to study at Central Bible College. And while I did not cash in on the offer, I did learn an early lesson about God's favor.

If you apply the principles of God's favor, keeping them foremost in your life, His blessings will follow. But it takes intent; it takes preparation; it takes planning.

A successful favor action plan addresses family; your work, business, or schooling; and your Christian life of faithfulness, diligence, and integrity. And it is all bathed in prayer, even as that plan is playing out.

Living a life of favor takes intent,
preparation, and planning.

In the second chapter of the Book of Nehemiah, our cupbearer confessed he was afraid but prepared. Quietly, he entered the throne room to serve wine to Artaxerxes and his queen—wine Nehemiah had tested with his own lips to guard against poison.

You can imagine how the plan may have begun to play out. With a bow, Nehemiah presents the cup, drawing near enough for the king to see how drawn his trusted servant's face was; perhaps he would even notice the redness of swollen eyes.

The kings says, "Why does your face look so sad when you are not ill? This can be nothing but sadness of heart" (Neh. 2:2).

Perhaps Nehemiah gulped. Maybe he took a long, deep breath. It was a dangerous thing to look discontented in the king's presence. Ever fearful of assassination, the monarch might find a disturbed, unhappy face on his most trusted of servants sufficient cause for alarm—perhaps even cautionary execution.

But Nehemiah knew he had the king's favorable attention and that he had been given a sympathetic invitation to share his heart's longing.

"May the king live forever! Why should my face not look sad when the city where my fathers are buried lies in ruins, and its gates have been destroyed by fire?" Nehemiah cried out. And Artaxerxes, his heart softened, asked, "What is it you want?" (Neh 2:3–4).

The moment Nehemiah had prayed for and planned for had come. He knew what he said next could quickly turn his audience with the king from lament to action. There could be no wasting of this period of favor, this assigned advantage. He must ask for everything he would need—and Nehemiah had planned and likely listed and memorized these details ahead of time.

Scripture tells us that at this critical moment Nehemiah prayed. It was probably a short prayer, likely one seeking reassurance. Maybe it was something like what you or I might toss up to heaven between pounding heartbeats: "O Lord, this is it! Here we go!"

Straight to the point, Nehemiah then asked Artaxerxes to send him to Jerusalem for the specific mission of rebuilding the city—not just a temple, but homes, public buildings, gates, and walls.

Artaxerxes still could say no. After all, his cupbearer was asking him to reverse his earlier decision to halt reconstruction of Jerusalem's walls. But Nehemiah had the favor of God and, in answer to prayer, the favor of the king. There was no waning in Artaxerxes' compassion for this servant he had grown to respect and trust with his very life.

> *If you are going to be successful in putting together your plan to live and succeed under the banner of God's favor, you too must plan for "yes."*

"How long will your journey take, and when will you get back?" the king asked. As the cupbearer would later write in Nehemiah 2:6, "It pleased the king to send me; so I set a time."

And now, the planning kicked in. Nehemiah had plotted his course and what he would need with the same efficiency as he secured the king's food, drink, and safety.

First off, remembering the empire's bureaucrats who had waged the smear campaign that halted reconstruction of Jerusalem, he wanted to make sure there could be no misunderstanding that Artaxerxes had literally assigned advantage to Nehemiah in carrying out his mission.

> If it pleases the king, may I have letters to the governors of Trans-Euphrates, so that

> they will provide me safe-conduct until I
> arrive in Judah? And may I have a letter to
> Asaph, keeper of the king's forest, so he will
> give me timber to make beams for the gates
> of the citadel by the temple and for the city
> wall and for the residence I will occupy?
> —NEHEMIAH 2:7–8

Artaxerxes wanted to bless Nehemiah. The heart of a king changed from anti-Semitic to God's most powerful human instrument (whether he knew it or not; remember, Pharaoh, though much more stubborn, ended up serving God's purposes in freeing the Israelites of Exodus)—and one who would sweep away opposition with an edict.

Artaxerxes gave Nehemiah all he asked for, and more: an armed escort of cavalry to make sure that if the foes of the Jews weren't convinced by the letters from the king, the gleam of sword, spear, and shield would compel obedience.

First, Nehemiah prayed. Second, he planned for the favor of God to be granted, the blessing that exceeds what we know to ask and pours out of the coffers of heaven to meet needs we cannot see or dared not to imagine. Third, during that period of fasting and prayer, Nehemiah had given thought to provision for his mission so he wouldn't be stammering for an answer when the king asked him exactly what he needed.

If you are going to be successful in putting together your plan to live and succeed under the banner of God's favor, you too must plan for "yes."

How many times have you heard someone dreamily say, "I have this great idea"? Perhaps it is an invention or a means to provide ministry where obstacles have thwarted previous efforts, or perhaps it is some mission the person feels called to take on for God.

Then you ask the dreamer how, if the means were suddenly available, they would proceed; what would be the first, second, or third step?

An answer of "I don't know" or a blank stare won't win God's favor, will it?

So, first you pray. Planning follows, an expression of faith through positive action, through visualizing how God's blessing can be implemented best. Seeking sufficient provision grows naturally from planning.

The next step: expect and watch for progress, even as you begin the work.

It isn't always convenient. Our former ministry at Bayside Church in Green Bay did not start as much more than a strong call and yearning to see new souls brought to the Lord. Jan and I weren't looking to just start another evangelical church in Wisconsin where bored Christians from other congregations would gather; we wanted to attract those who had long ago let their faith wither, those who had never truly heard the gospel, and those for whom church as usual had no attraction.

But most of all, we wanted to see the so-called unchurched find a welcoming environment to be courted by the Spirit of Christ, accept Him, and grow in service to each other and the world outside our doors.

We had pastored successful churches in Wisconsin, Utah, and Oregon, and now we felt strongly called to Green Bay. I was forty-six at the time, but Jan and I agreed that this move was of God. In faith, we cashed in everything we had but the equity of our home and moved.

> *God is favor. He gives the vision, you step out with faith and a plan for successful service.*

Our first service was in August 1992 at Lombardi Middle School. We had 116 in the seats that first Sunday. We also had God's favor. The seats filled, and soon we needed bigger, more permanent facilities.

In the spring of 1994, we moved into the new Bayside Church building. A year and a half later, we added youth and children's ministry facilities and office space. The congregation grew from hundreds past a thousand, then two thousand. In April 1997, Bayside's campus opened forty thousand more square feet, including a new, larger sanctuary and rooms for our growing church ministries.

In 2005, we added a 500-seat auditorium for our growing youth program and renovated the main sanctuary as our attendance continued to grow and was accommodated in multiple services. And, true to the calling God gave Jan and me, about 80 percent of those adherents first experienced Christ at Bayside.

Through monetary and other aid, our church also has been able to reach out to Christians in countries where their faith is often an invitation to persecution, sometimes even death—places like India, Nepal, Bangladesh, Myanmar, China, Saudi Arabia, and countries in Africa.

God's favor. He gives the vision, and you step out with faith and a plan for successful service.

That's what Nehemiah did when, with the favor of God and king fully behind him, he arrived with his entourage in Jerusalem.

> "You see the trouble we are in: Jerusalem lies in ruins, and its gates have been burned with fire. Come, let us rebuild the wall of Jerusalem, and we will no longer be in disgrace." I also told them about the gracious hand of my God upon me and what the king had said to me. They replied, "Let us start rebuilding." So they began this good work.
>
> —NEHEMIAH 2:17–18

Huddled in the rubble, open to raids from their enemies, the Jews of Jerusalem had begun to lose hope. But now, here came Nehemiah with the king's letters, soldiers to enforce the orders and protect the mission—and hope.

Just as important, perhaps more so at that moment of arrival, Nehemiah had a plan, and provisions were streaming into the ruined city. When the revitalized Jews of Jerusalem asked what to do next, he had the answers; they could visualize how this could actually happen, after all.

They had a new vision—Nehemiah's. In effect, their answer back to his carefully laid plans was a heartfelt, "Let's do it!"

Persistent petitions by two men of faith and integrity had been honored by God: Ezra the priest, whose heart yearned for a revival within the Jewish remnant, and Nehemiah, the cupbearer to a king, who called on God's intervention from a grief as deep as his soul to rebuild both physical and spiritual Jerusalem.

More of that favor would be needed. Satan and his human minions back in Judah were defeated, but their hatred remained. The walls and gates had finally begun to rise again, but the opposition had not disappeared.

Then, as now, one way to know for sure if you are being an effective servant of God is how much opposition you attract. Nehemiah knew that and, in faith, prepared both spiritually and practically for the Lord to act.

When you live for and seek God's favor, put your plan together, and begin to implement it, step by step, you will begin to see progress, too. At home, on the job, and in every part of your life make the Lord your top priority.

That's how, even in the midst of the most evil environment, you can shine. God will bless your workplace, your family, your church, and your dreams because He sees His servants living lives of principle and truth.

Chapter 6

OPPOSITION— THE PROOF OF FAVOR

"All who live godly in Christ Jesus shall suffer persecution."

W E HAVE ALL been there: you get on a roll and are doing things right, and then, *boom!* Here comes the opposition. If you are honest, you think, if not actually pray, "Lord, what's this all about?"

Just as surely as a shadow proves the existence of light and a total eclipse demonstrates the reality of our solar system's sun, opposition is a certain sign that God's favor rests on your life—and that the enemies of truth know it.

Simply put, if someone isn't attacking you, there is a good chance you are not doing anything that is worth worrying the opposition. Godly living will bring conviction; making decisions based on the Bible's teachings, integrity, and holiness will stir up problems. It is supposed to work that way.

Doing things God's way does not shield you from attacks, but if you stand strong, trust, and pray, the Lord promises victory.

> *If someone isn't attacking you, there is a good chance you are not doing anything that is worth worrying the opposition.*

Your opposition will come from those who reject the work of God, from those who are angry at being reminded by your example and steadfast living that sin exists and that they are in rebellion against their Maker. Others will be jealous of the success favor brings to your life—and once again, I am not talking necessarily about money here.

God may very well choose to provide monetary resources to you—as a steward entrusted to, in turn, invest it in His work. But more often, that favor, God's assigned advantage, comes in more precious areas of life: good kids who love God, your own blossoming spiritual life and joy, a blessed marriage, and a great work ethic that brings the favor of man, too.

Opposition most certainly comes from the enemy of our souls—Satan and his spiritual realm of rebellion and deceit. This opponent has not ceased his offensive against humankind since the fall of Adam and Eve; he wanted to destroy the perfect environment of the Garden of Eden, and he did.

Now, the enemy wants to destroy the working of God's favor in your life. Want proof? Besides your own struggles with sin and doubt, just look around. We are embroiled in a battle of secular versus spiritual cultures. In America today, we talk more about tolerance rather than the truth. If you stand up for what is right, see how accepting the self-professed tolerance advocates are toward you.

Yes, God wants us to be a people who are compassionate and accepting of others, leaving judgment to Him. He also wants us to be a people of integrity, able to stand for the truth in order to also be a people He can bless.

So, be forewarned. The opposition will come, if you are living for God's favor. Here are some of the forms those attacks will take and how we can learn to meet them, according to our old friend Nehemiah.

First may come an assault on the credibility of your work.

> When Sanballat heard that we were rebuilding the wall, he became angry and was greatly incensed. He ridiculed the Jews, and in the presence of his associates and the army of Samaria, he said, "What are those feeble Jews doing? Will they restore their wall? Will they offer sacrifices? Will they finish in a day? Can they bring stones back to life from those heaps of rubble—burned as they are?'
>
> Tobiah the Ammonite, who was at his side, said, "What they are building—if

even a fox climbed up on it, he would break down their wall of stones!"

—NEHEMIAH 4:1–3

When Nehemiah heard this, he responded with a tough, no compromise attitude. I call it his "Dirty Harry Prayer." You probably remember actor Clint Eastwood's portrayal of the gritty San Francisco police Lt. Harry Callahan—and that hand cannon of a revolver he carried.

> *You are going to be attacked if you live a life worthy of God's favor. Count on it.*

In the 1983 movie *Sudden Impact* Eastwood's character interrupts the robbery of a diner. He quickly guns down two of the robbers, and when the third takes a waitress hostage at gunpoint, "Harry" calmly points his own revolver directly at the criminal's face.

"Go ahead. Make my day," he says with a mad glint in his eye. The robber hesitates and then surrenders.

Instead of a gun, Nehemiah unholstered a powerful prayer. You can feel the heat behind the words.

> Hear us, O our God, for we are despised. Turn their insults back on their own heads. Give them over as plunder in a land of captivity. Do not cover up their guilt or blot out their sins from your sight, for they have thrown insults in the face of the builders.
> —NEHEMIAH 4:4–5

You are going to be attacked if you live a life worthy of God's favor. Count on it. As we work to build the church of Christ, as we live good, quality lives, dedicate our work and workplaces to excellence, and take stands on moral grounds, we will become targets. You will become a target. Like Nehemiah, you just have to stand up.

And when you do that, the attacks of anger, characterized by evil scheming, may very well be the next things you face. Our courageous cupbearer certainly did.

> But when Sanballat, Tobiah, the Arabs, the Ammonites and the men of Ashdod heard that the repairs to Jerusalem's walls had gone ahead and that the gaps were being closed, they were very angry. They all plotted together to come and fight against Jerusalem and stir up trouble against it.
>
> —NEHEMIAH 4:7–8

Nehemiah's answer was prayer—and preparation. He and his Jewish friends prayed for God's protection, and they posted armed guards day and night to keep a lookout.

But while acting to secure the city and their work from attack from enemies without, Nehemiah and company found the discouraging words of the naysayers within their ranks to be just as great a challenge. "Wherever you turn, they will attack us," they whined constantly in Nehemiah 4:12.

Add to that, the workers on the wall were growing fatigued; just the arduous task of clearing away the rubble was enormous, let alone rebuilding the wall while worried about being suddenly attacked.

Nehemiah's response could have been, "All right, I've had it. I'm going back to Susa. Yep, I had me a really good job there, and they want me back. I'm outta here!"

No. Instead, he met the threats from outside and inside with a show of determination and force. By family units, he armed men with swords, spears, and bows to defend the weak points of the rising wall. Then he rallied them with words of faith and strength.

"Don't be afraid of them. Remember the Lord, who is great and awesome, and fight for your brothers, your sons and your daughters, your wives and your homes," Nehemiah told them in Nehemiah 4:14.

The enemy—seeing God's people alert, prepared, and ready to fight—had no heart for battle, and the campaign was derailed before it could start. Nonetheless, Nehemiah kept his guard up; half the men worked, swords at their sides, while the other half was fully on guard.

There is a critically important point in this for

all who would live for God's favor. It is simply this: never, ever let your guard down.

Consider Nehemiah's working warriors. Our God will fight for us, but we must do our part. So, we need to have the sword of the Spirit in one hand—the power of the Word of God, the dynamic of the Holy Spirit working in us constantly—and with the other hand do the work.

You need what you have in both hands. Drop your sword, and you are defenseless; drop your work, and you are unbalanced. In God's army, an empty-handed soldier is ineffective, useless in battle or in working to build the kingdom. There is always another battle to win, another breach in the wall to repair.

> *God will fight for us, but we must do our part: the sword of the Spirit in one hand, and with the other hand do the work.*

History is full of battles won but wars lost because armies relaxed and thus became easy targets for counterattacks. It is the same with our spiritual warfare; we must always be preparing for the next battle.

There is an old hymn, penned in 1858 by George Duffield Jr. but still sung today, that expresses the sentiment well:

> Stand up, stand up for Jesus, ye soldiers of the cross;
> Lift high His royal banner, it must not suffer loss.
> From vict'ry unto vict'ry His army shall He lead,
> Till every foe is vanquished and Christ is Lord indeed.[1]

We need victory after victory in raising families that love God and honor His principles—mothers, fathers, and children who show the way to salvation and grace to the lost. We need victories in the office, on the loading dock, or wherever you work; in the classroom; and on those nights when the worries of the day crowd our minds and rob us of peaceful sleep.

Sometimes, we need victory in the form of courage and faith for the long haul. An example of this is my friend Tim Johnson, a high school band director. He will tell you: God's favor shines even in the midst of life's nightmares.

On February 20, 2002, Tim's doctor uttered those nightmarish words: "You have cancer." It had taken one of the disease's most deadly forms, multiple myeloma, or bone cancer. With treatment, the doctor said, Tim might squeeze in another two years of life; without treatment, he had just months left.

Tim finally had an explanation for the exhaustion and constant aches and pains he had endured already for a year. But there was more bad news: a bugling disk in his spine was pressing against his sciatic nerve. This disorder was too far along for surgery due to the risk of damaging his spinal cord.

As if those crises weren't enough, doctors also had found that Tim's hip and femur (thigh bone) were literally disintegrating. Already, the bone mass in the afflicted areas had been reduced by roughly 50 percent.

Telling his wife, Joan, and the rest of his family of the diagnoses, they decided that instead of a prayer of desperation they would unite in taking the matter to the Lord with a simple petition emphasizing love, God's authority over illness, submission to His will, and even praise.

"It was a prayer that still amazes me and often causes me to well up with tears," Tim says now. "All they expressed to God was trust. My dad said something that carried me through what would prove to be two and a half years of constant battling to survive."

"The question isn't whether God will be with you, but whether you'll stay with God," Tim's father told him. "Don't ever forget God already knows how this will turn out, and if you trust Him, it will be for the good."

The next day, Tim stood before his band students to tell them of the cancer. First, there was stunned silence. Then one girl raised her hand. "Can I give you a hug?" she asked. As Tim wept, one student after another came forward to embrace him and offer encouragement. Many of them thanked him for little things he had done to lift them up and told him how they admired his Christian faith.

> *Our warfare—in sickness or in health—is not only us against spiritual darkness and demonic suggestions to surrender and compromise, but it is also us gritting our teeth and holding on to what is true and right.*

As the news spread, many students—inside the band and throughout the school—returned to church to pray for their beloved teacher. Parents wrote Tim notes about spontaneous student Bible studies springing up.

"It was becoming clear I didn't get cancer because I was cursed or had committed some big sin that God was punishing me for," Tim says he realized. "He was using it to give me a voice. For years I'd been praying that God would give me a greater opportunity to share my faith with the students, and now—because of the cancer—I had that opportunity."

Tim would need all the assurance and prayers he received. After weeks of chemotherapy he could hardly get out of bed, even to go to the bathroom. He became so weak that relieving himself became an arduous journey; a few steps became a marathon, one requiring a long period of rest midway before shuffling back to his bed.

Depression set in. He felt "totally worthless… a nuisance and a burden to everyone in my life, especially my wife and two young sons." The pain that kept him awake at nights was matched by the anguish inside his mind. He had tried to serve God all of his life, and this is what he got in return? Tim felt God had abandoned him.

At his lowest point, when even forming the words of prayer seemed too much effort, Tim found his turning point. One word. One person. The only answer. "Jesus," he rasped. And again, "Jesus." It was as far as his mind could go. He was clinging to that name. "Jesus. Jesus. Jesus."

"Jesus was the only positive thought in my mind," Tim recalls now. "I'd think, 'I'm worthless.' Then, 'Jesus. Just die. Jesus.' Looking back on it, I realize it was the power of the name of Jesus versus the power of darkness."

The next thing he knew, Tim was waking up, having slept through the remainder of that pivotal night. The depression was gone; he felt upbeat—and convinced God was with him and that he could trust Him completely.

The following days saw his strength returning. He not only made the trips to the bathroom, but he also got supplies and began cleaning the fixtures. At first, he'd take a pillow with him, resting his head on the toilet seat. "I was no longer worthless. I could help Joan," he remembers.

As his health returned, Tim made frequent trips back to his high school to give students and faculty friends updates and his testimony of serving the Lord in one of life's worst storms.

It has been nearly five years since Tim got that dire news from his doctors that he had, at best, two years to live. As of this writing, he is back to work and serving the Lord.

Like Nehemiah, Tim came to realize that our warfare—in sickness or in health—is not only us against spiritual darkness and demonic suggestions to surrender and compromise, but it is also us gritting our teeth and holding on to what is true and right.

We also must guard our integrity, as individuals and as bodies of believers, as the cupbearer instructed in Nehemiah 5:1–12. Nehemiah recounted yet another crisis confronting his mission: the work of God was progressing with brick and mortar, but in the hearts of some of Jerusalem's Jewish settlers, arrogance, greed, and lack of compassion had taken root.

The rich got richer; the poor got poorer. To feed their families and pay exorbitant taxes, poor Jews were selling what they had to their better-off brothers—fields, vineyards, and even their homes. Some were so desperate they sold their sons and daughters into slavery to neighboring Gentiles. Nehemiah rescued as many as he could, only to see them sold again to pay on their increasing debt to their wealthier brothers.

This was a truly vicious circle, but Nehemiah called the wrongdoers to account, and the convicting power of God's Spirit no doubt drove home the message to hardened hearts.

"What you are doing is not right. Shouldn't you walk in the fear of our God to avoid the reproach of our Gentile enemies? I and my brothers are and my men are also lending the people money and grain.

But let the exacting of usury [interest] stop!" Nehemiah told them.

You do not profit from violating God's principles. The wrongdoers, chastised, voluntarily returned the property and homes they had taken—and the interest they had charged as well. They even took an oath before the Lord that they would not return to their old ways.

Nehemiah's own unswerving example of integrity and the evidence of God's favor that obviously came with it put him in a position where he could exhort his errant brothers without his own character being undercut by hypocrisy.

This was a perfect time for the enemy to attack Nehemiah through his ego; he was on top of his game, his fame growing with each victory. But he was on guard for this, too, keeping himself humbled before God.

Past governors had winked at and perhaps even shared in the profits of mistreatment of the rank-and-file Jews of Jerusalem. Nehemiah could have done so as well; who would challenge him, with the support he had from Artaxerxes?

Instead, for twelve years running, Nehemiah and his brothers made it the practice to open up their tables to others instead of hoarding the food specially allotted by the king to his governor. Nehemiah did not add maintenance of his household to the burden of the people and did not take advantage of what we today would call a "buyer's market" in real estate sold by distressed families.

And so, he could pray a blessing upon himself and his family that for others would be an act of arrogance. Nehemiah knew his life had been lived by God's favor and that the Lord had promised assigned favor for His servants who lived by heavenly principles.

Once again, though, Nehemiah reminds us that the enemy never sleeps. Having failed with threats of military attack, seen their whispering and fear-mongering campaigns fail, and finally witnessing the new unity of Jerusalem through the Jewish nobles' repentance from sin, Nehemiah's foes turned to the strategy of ambush.

> When word came to Sanballat, Tobiah, Geshem the Arab and the rest of our enemies

that I had rebuilt the wall and not a gap was left in it...[they] sent me this message: "Come, let us meet together in one of the villages on the plain of Ono." But they were scheming to harm me; so I sent messengers to them with this reply: "I am carrying on a great project and cannot go down. Why should the work stop while I leave it and go down to you?"

—Nehemiah 6:1–3

Scripture tells us that Sanballat and his minions tried variations of the same scheme—to get Nehemiah outside the walls of Jerusalem, away from his base of support—four more times. Each of these hidden invitations to assassination was turned down with the same words.

According to Nehemiah 6:6–7, his exasperated foes finally resorted to naked extortion:

It is reported...that you and the Jews are plotting to revolt, and therefore you are building the wall. Moreover, according to these reports you are about to become their king and have even appointed prophets to make this proclamation about you in Jerusalem: "There is a king in Judah!"

These lies came in the form of an unsealed letter. The intention was obvious. Just in case the threat wasn't clear, though, they spelled it out: "Now this report will get back to the king; so come, let us confer together" (v. 7).

Truth is, a copy of the accusations probably had already been sent back to Susa. What better excuse, they could later argue to Artaxerxes, for killing this "traitorous" Jew, and hadn't they tried to warn the king?

Nehemiah knew, though, that God had brought him this far and would see his work through. And the cupbearer Nehemiah knew of the special trust he had built up with Artaxerxes, too. He had the favor of God and king; nothing would shake either.

First, Nehemiah went on record denying their charges, and he let his accusers know he knew who was truly behind the lies. Then he prayed for God's strength to go forward. Confirmation for his faithful steps came when his enemies next bribed a local soothsayer to "warn" Nehemiah of a plot to kill him by night.

"Let us meet in the house of God, inside the temple, and let us close the temple doors, because men are coming to kill you," said Shemaiah son of Delaiah (Neh. 6:10).

Nehemiah's answer was unflinching: "Why should a man like me, one so blessed by God and king, run away and hide, even to save his life? I will not go!" he said.

Nehemiah knew that following the cunning advice of this false prophet would be a sin against all God had accomplished and would tarnish the name of the Lord's appointed leader at an important milestone in Jewish history.

We too seek God's favor in our lives. We invite Him to grant us that assigned advantage against the foes of the gospel, the enemies of right living, and those who oppose strong, God-fearing families and Christians whose quiet faith is openly adorned with integrity.

And like Nehemiah, we are not going to run when opposition comes our way. We will stand, we will pray for promised favor, and we will know that attacks from the enemy are the price—and the shadows of victory to come—for living life God's way.

Chapter 7

FAVOR, FOREVER

Staying strong, consistent, and faithful

N ANY JOURNEY, you can best gain perspective by taking a break at the summit of the trail, taking a deep breath, and looking back to where you have been. Let's do that now.

Together we have followed the path of faith mapped out in this book. It is a trail broken long ago by a Jewish slave boy who rose to be the most trusted adviser of a king—the cupbearer Nehemiah. We saw how he humbled himself to receive great favor from God and man. And we learned how Nehemiah dared to pray, with a practiced confidence, prepared to risk his standing and perhaps even his life for his people before Artaxerxes:

> O Lord, let your ear be attentive to the prayer of this your servant and to the prayer of your servants who delight in revering your name. Give your servant success today by granting him favor in the presence of this man.
>
> —NEHEMIAH 1:11

Together, we learned how to apply the favor prayer, with hope built on a principled lifestyle that legitimized our claim to God's assigned advantage. That lifestyle is one of dedicating ourselves to putting His purposes first—not just in church but on the job, at home in our relationships with spouses and children, and in our communities as neighbors, friends, and, most importantly, witnesses of God's grace.

To recap, we have discovered these truths:

- You must be diligent and live godly lives to gain God's favor, no matter what your environmental circumstances are.

- You must live a life of integrity if you expect God to respond to your prayer for favor. Integrity is the prerequisite for both receiving and responsibly applying the blessings that come from the assigned advantage of the Lord.

- Godly hard work will bring opposition. Remember? No sunlight without shadows.

I have never been one to proclaim that the Lord's return is a certain day and time. We have seen too much of this over the years, with people running off to some hilltop to punch their one-way rapture flight ticket to heaven.

Then comes the disappointment and, for some, a loss of what fragile faith they had. Fragile, I say, because had they read the Scriptures, they would have been able to discern a false prophet and counterfeit message. Jesus Himself told us that no one knows the day or hour of His return; only our Father God knows.

That said, I do believe the Lord's return for His people could occur any time now. We live in perilous times, prophetic times, and need to be ready. Still, we often are lulled into a dull sleepy state by the constant drum of news about unmerciful weather—earthquakes, mudslides, floods, tsunamis, and on and on. It becomes all too common news, too much to fathom and, eventually, just part of the fabric of a sad existence.

But we cannot sleep through this. These events should spur us on to greater compassion for those who do not yet know Christ! As God's children, bought with a horrible price in the blood and suffering of Jesus, we are responsible for giving the unsaved the opportunity to make informed decisions on their eternal welfare.

In the life of favor, sharing the gospel is the only road to success by God's standards. Witnessing, yes. Standing up for what is right when the crowd would just rather turn away? Of course. But we also share the good news of salvation and restoration by example—living lives that convey godly principles and the blessings of peace and love to our families, co-workers, and neighbors.

> *The favor of God comes from hard work and moral diligence in all circumstances.*

First, we pray. It must come from a humbled, but confident heart. God wants our passion, that spiritual flame that responds to the breathing in of His words by flaring into a bonfire of the soul, the kind that beckons the lost from darkness and offers the warmth of love and forgiveness.

Prayer is not magic; it is not some incantation muttered from some book that results in fairy dust being sprinkled on you. It just does not happen that way.

The favor of God comes from hard work and moral diligence in all circumstances. This prepares the way for prayer—and when you pray, let it be all about Him and His purposes. Sure, you can pray for your needs, but those things are always best met while uncompromisingly in His service.

For Nehemiah, the purpose was to restore Jerusalem's wall, which signified the unity and strength of God's people. Our "wall" challenge today is reaching the lost. We do that best by living in favor before them, exhibiting lives that stir hope in those looking for answers in their own.

It has to be real. People today are used to being lied to, misled, and conned by those claiming to have only their welfare as their concern. For many, the first instinct when meeting a purported "Christian" businessman is not to listen but to grab their wallets and run.

> *To continue in the flow of God's favor, you must keep God's words as the centerpiece of your life.*

It doesn't matter that the vast majority of believers in business, or any other profession, strive to conduct their affairs fairly and honestly. It only takes one bad experience to sour a nonbeliever's perception of what it means to be a Christian. That makes it so much more difficult to share the gospel with that person—but of course, through the ministry of the Holy Spirit, all things are possible.

So, you are one who gets it. You strive to be a man or woman of integrity, and you put Christ first in your life. You yearn for God's favor to be a powerfully effective servant of the kingdom. Your prayers for this assigned advantage have brought evidence of that favor at work, in the home, and in new, exciting ways to serve Him.

How do you ensure the continuing flow of favor in your life? I believe the Lord has shown us seven principles to do just that.

1. Give God the credit.

This was a clear, primary factor in Nehemiah's life and in the lives of all the patriarchs of faith. In Nehemiah 6:15, the cupbearer tells us it took fifty-two days to rebuild Jerusalem's walls! This is an amazing feat, given the opposition the city's Jewish remnant faced from powerful enemies and the task alone of clearing away decades of rubble.

We all could understand if Nehemiah was just a little bit proud of this accomplishment. And it must have been personally gratifying to him to learn how completing the wall had knocked his foes back on their heels.

"When all our enemies heard about this, all the surrounding nations were afraid and lost their self-confidence," the scripture recounts.

What comes next? Did Nehemiah write something akin to, "In your face, Sanballat! Who's the man? Yo, pagan, you're lookin' at him!" No. But if we're honest, a lot of us would have said, or at least thought, something along those lines.

Instead, Nehemiah completes his account of that episode this way. He wrote that the enemies of God's people "lost their self-confidence, because they realized that this work had been done *with the help of our God*" (Neh. 6:16, emphasis added).

It was a corporate effort, a precursor of the body of Christ all believers make up. God gave favor to Nehemiah and the mission special to his heart. That followed with assigned advantage in planning, equipping, and protecting the project. Then God's people heard the words of Nehemiah, faith and determination flared in their hearts, and it was time to go to work.

2. If you want to continue in the flow of God's favor, you must keep God's words as the center-piece of your life.

For most Christians, that simply is not the case. Survey after survey reveals the average Christian spends more time reading the sports page or magazines and watching television than they ever do in reading the Bible.

What kind of friendship or marriage could survive such neglect? And yet, there is no relationship more important than that with your Creator. God's Word has to be the core of your heart; there, the Holy Spirit interprets it to your life, shining the light of understanding on those passages formerly mysterious or meaningless to you.

> *Something very special happens within the corporate worship and message times the church provides.*

Time and neglect had made the Scriptures vague and forgotten to Jerusalem's Jews in Nehemiah's time. He called on Ezra, the priest God had used earlier to lead the remnant back to the City of David to rebuild the temple, to read the Law of Moses to a great gathering in the city's main square.

As the law was read, the people were convicted of their sins. They listened, they understood, and they wept. There was repentance in hearts that day. Finally, Nehemiah joined Ezra; together they shared God's forgiveness, and mourning turned to celebration.

> Then all the people went away to eat and drink, to send portions of food and to celebrate with great joy, because they now understood the words that had been made known to them.
> —NEHEMIAH 8:12

Five hundred years later, another man of favor, the apostle John, wrote down the words of Jesus along the same line:

If you hold to my teaching, you are really
my disciples. Then you will know the truth,
and the truth will set you free.

—JOHN 8:31–32

**3. Maintaining a heart tender toward our Lord,
one that is always ready to worship and express
thanksgiving, flows logically from living a God-
centered life.**

Nehemiah 12:27 paints a picture of godly celebration at the dedication of the wall of Jerusalem with
"the music of cymbals, harps and lyres." Singers were
recruited from Jerusalem and all the new villages that
had sprung up under the newly provided protection
of its sturdy walls.

Something very special to the Lord—and to our
own spiritual welfare—happens within the corporate
worship and message times of Sunday services, the
midweek prayer and Bible study meetings, and the
youth activities the church provides. We are joined
in our love for Christ and God's Word, setting aside
time to learn, celebrate, and listen.

Have a heart for worship, whatever form that takes. In the evangelical movement, worship can be energetic and exuberant. People raise their hands; they may even dance. Other believers feel more natural in quieter praise, more structured and corporate forms of thanksgiving.

God honors all of these expressions, as they honestly reveal the hearts of His children. We are made wonderfully different from each other! Imagine that day when we are ushered into the presence of our Lord; have you ever wondered about how you will react?

Will you fall flat upon your face in awe? Will you kiss the Savior's nail-scarred feet or sob in joy holding His pierced hands? Or will you be swept up in the embrace of Him who gave all for you—the Nazarene who died that you might have the Father's favor and not His eternal rejection?

4. Keep your spiritual house clean.

Another word for this principle is sanctification. Whatever you call it, it is an ongoing process because we live daily in a polluted world—not just the physical environment, but also the moral and spiritual environment. What we see on TV and what we read and hear just in the course of a "normal" day can and does leave behind stains and dirt on our souls.

Immersing ourselves daily in the Word of God is the spiritual equivalent of a daily shower or bath. Neither dirt nor sinful influences and moral pollution come off without regular cleansing.

In Nehemiah 13:6–7, we learn that Nehemiah had returned to Artaxerxes' court to give a report, and then he later returned to Jerusalem, only to find that a priest by the name of Eliashib had turned over a large room in the temple complex to a friend, Tobiah, for his personal use. That room had been set aside earlier for the specific purpose of storing grain offerings, incense, and temple articles as well as tithes intended to provision the Levites, singers, priest, and others dedicated to serving the house of God.

> *Immersing ourselves daily in the Word of God is the spiritual equivalent of a daily shower or bath.*

Nehemiah, "greatly displeased," evicted Tobiah and had the household goods he had stored in the room tossed out. He then had the holy storage space purified and had the appropriate tithes, offerings, and temple items returned to their proper place.

Next, he learned the Levites in particular had suffered in his absence. From the time of Moses, God had ordained that because the Levites were dedicated to maintaining the tabernacle and later the temple, they would receive provisions from the tithes and offerings the people presented instead of real estate in the Promised Land.

But when Nehemiah returned from the king's court, he learned the Levites had been forced to work in the fields to make ends meet. He rebuked the officials in charge of this: "'Why is the house of God neglected?' Then I called them [the Levites] together and stationed them at their posts" (Neh. 13:11).

The boss was back in town, and the Jewish community responded by restoring the tithes and offerings needed for the priestly class to have food on their tables as they did God's work. To make sure things stayed the way they should, Nehemiah cleaned out the old management and put a trusted trio—one a priest, another a scribe, and the third a Levite—in charge.

Everyone needs a trusted friend to periodically offer critical, constructive analysis of his or her life. This helps you keep on top of that spiritual house-cleaning mentioned earlier.

And I am convinced that if you keep yourself clean—mentally, spiritually, and physically—you will not only obtain God's special favor, but you will also keep it. There is no rest in this battle, either. The enemy can find your weakness at any age, if you open the wrong doors to your heart to temptation or compromise.

5. Do not forsake the house of God.

For Nehemiah, that meant safeguarding the holiness of temple spaces and providing the ordained grain, wine, and meat offerings God had set aside for the tables of His servants.

Today, this means to not forsake our Christian community gatherings. Sunday is the day we have designated for nearly two thousand years as our time to meet, worship, and minister. We also are fortunate that our modern churches provide Bible studies, prayer groups, and many ministries to serve the needs of our communities—inside and outside the doors of our sanctuaries. This flows into the sixth point.

6. Keep God's commands.

Sounds pretty straightforward, doesn't it? But even after all they had accomplished with God's blessings and protection, the people of Nehemiah's Jerusalem slid into sin—specifically, violating the Sabbath.

Nehemiah 13:15–16 recounts how the cupbearer found the people working their winepresses and loading their donkeys for the trip to markets in Jerusalem. The God-ordained day of rest and reflection had given way to commerce. Even pagans from Tyre were hauling in fish and merchandise to sell in the City of David.

> I rebuked the nobles of Judah and said to them, "What is this wicked thing you are doing—desecrating the Sabbath day? Didn't your forefathers do the same things, so that our God brought down all this calamity

upon us and upon this city? Now you are stirring up more wrath against Israel by desecrating the Sabbath."

—Nehemiah 13:17–18

Nehemiah ordered the city's gates shut during the Sabbath and placed his own men on guard to make sure the orders were followed. He then ordered the Levites to purify themselves and take over the duty of enforcing the Sabbath's ban on work and trade.

Today we are not under the Law of Moses, though the principles God laid down in the commandments and through the inspired words of His Son and disciples should engender the same devotion. In other words, if you know something is right, do it; if you know it is wrong, don't.

Simply put, if God said it, I will obey it. That is a hard-and-fast rule on the road to godly favor.

7. Keep your family pure so they too can experience God's assigned advantage.

In Nehemiah 13:23–30, Nehemiah found that intermarriage with neighboring pagans had become rampant. Half of the children of such unions didn't even speak Hebrew, let alone know about the God of Israel. The very survival of the nation was at stake with this threatened dilution of Jewish blood and culture, and Nehemiah acted decisively, to say the least.

> I rebuked them and called curses down on them. I beat some of the men and pulled out their hair. I made them take an oath in God's name and said: "You are not to give your daughters in marriage to their sons, nor are you to take their daughters in marriage for your sons or for yourselves."
> —NEHEMIAH 13:25

Nehemiah knew Israel had been down this path before. King Solomon had sown the seeds of his kingdom's eventual division and decline by bringing in hundreds of foreign, idol-worshiping women to his harem. His lust was a flaw in his renowned wisdom, and Israel suffered from the example.

We too should make sure that when we marry, it is to spouses of like and precious faith. With our children, too, we should take every opportunity for them to benefit from activities that reinforce godly training outside the family. And when they date, we must have the courage as parents to keep them from nonbelievers.

Oh, your popularity with that daughter or son may bottom out, but it is a fight worth waging for the future happiness of your children. Take a stand.

This principle extends beyond romance, too. Watch your alliances—friendships, business partnerships. You need to be on the same page spiritually, involved with godly people.

This is the life of favor. You must be all about the things of God, concerned with the lost. Apply the principles of integrity, humility, obedience, prayer, and worship day in and day out, week after week, year after year.

If the Rapture occurred right now, have you been the kind of parent, church member, employee or employer, husband or wife God would be honored to know? Have you shared the good news of Christ with the people in your sphere of influence?

Change your attitude if the answers to any of those questions is no. Get involved in life; allow favor to flow into your spirit. If we all did this, we could not build enough church buildings fast enough to hold all those who would come to the Lord.

We have to start living the Word of God. Then we too can pray Nehemiah's prayer: "O Lord, let your ear be attentive to the prayer of this your servant and to the prayer of your servants who delight in revering your name."

> *This is the life of favor: to be all about the things of God, concerned with the lost, applying the principles of integrity, humility, obedience, prayer, and worship day in and day out, week after week, year after year.*

It is up to us.

Notes

CHAPTER 3
FIRST, YOU PRAY

1. Gerald Friedman, "The End of Leisure?" *Econ-Atrocity Bulletin*, September 5, 2003, http://www.fguide.org/Bulletin/leisure.htm (accessed January 25, 2007).

2. U.S. Department of Labor, Bureau of Labor Statistics, "American Time Use Survey—2004 Results Announced by BLS," http://www.bls.gov/news.release/archives/atus_09202005.pdf (accessed February 26, 2007).

CHAPTER 4
PARTNERSHIP—A VISION IN COMMON

1. Booker T. Washington, *Up From Slavery* (N.p.: Adamant Media Corporation, 2006), 32.

2. TopicSites.com, "Booker T. Washington Quotes," http://www.topicsites.com/booker -t-washington/booker-t-washington-quotes .htm (accessed January 25, 2007).

3. Ibid.

4. John C. Maxwell, "Maxwell Moment: I'm 60 and Compounding," *Leadership Wired,* http://www.maximumimpact.com/ newsletters/leadership/content/issues/9_22/ default.htm (accessed February 26, 2007).

5. Radio-Television News Director Association and Foundation (RTNDA), Awards and Scholarships: 2002 RTNDA Edward R. Murrow Award Regional Winners, http:// www.rtnda.org/asfi/awards/2002regwinners .shtml#region4 (accessed February 26, 2007); also, KSTP.com, "Ryan Kibbe— Sports Reporter," http://www.kstp .com/article/stories/s10760.shtml?cat=28 (accessed February 26, 2007).

CHAPTER 6
OPPOSITION—THE PROOF OF FAVOR

1. "Stand Up, Stand Up for Jesus" by George Duffield Jr. Public domain.